S0-AZI-224

THE
MARKET
TAKER'S
EDGE

INSIDER STRATEGIES
FROM THE OPTIONS
TRADING FLOOR

THE
MARKET
TAKER'S
EDGE

DAN PASSARELLI

New York   Chicago   San Francisco   Lisbon
London   Madrid   Mexico City   Milan   New Delhi
San Juan   Seoul   Singapore   Sydney   Toronto

The *McGraw·Hill* Companies

Copyright © 2011 by The McGraw-Hill Companies, Inc. All rights reserved. Printed in the United States of America. Except as permitted under the United States Copyright Act of 1976, no part of this publication may be reproduced or distributed in any form or by any means, or stored in a database or retrieval system, without the prior written permission of the publisher.

1 2 3 4 5 6 7 8 9 10   QFR/QFR   1 9 8 7 6 5 4 3 2 1

ISBN   978-0-07-175492-7
MHID   0-07-175492-X

e-ISBN   978-0-07-175494-1
e-MHID 0-07-175494-6

This publication is designed to provide accurate and authoritative information in regard to the subject matter covered. It is sold with the understanding that neither the author nor the publisher is engaged in rendering legal, accounting, securities trading, or other professional services. If legal advice or other expert assistance is required, the services of a competent professional person should be sought.

—From a Declaration of Principles jointly adopted
by a Committee of the American Bar Association
and a Committee of Publishers and Associations

McGraw-Hill books are available at special quantity discounts to use as premiums and sales promotions or for use in corporate training programs. To contact a representative, please e-mail us at bulksales@mcgraw-hill.com.

This book is printed on acid-free paper.

To Kathleen, Sam, and Isabel

CONTENTS

FOREWORD

It is truly a new dawn in the options industry. Until recently, professional traders had two major advantages over nonprofessional, individual traders. Those advantages were technology and transaction costs. Computers and the Internet have largely eliminated the technology advantage, and this advancing technology has also brought down trading commissions for individual traders. Of equal importance is the multiple listing of options. Most options are traded—or listed—on several exchanges, and the resulting competition between exchanges and market makers has narrowed bid-ask spreads to the point to where professional traders no longer have an advantage.

But significant differences still exist between professionals and nonprofessionals, and it is essential that individual traders understand these differences. What the trading industry has needed is a book that brings professional-trading experience and real-world know-how to the self-directed, individual trader; that is what Dan Passarelli's book delivers. *The Market Taker's Edge: Insider Strategies from the Options Trading Floor* provides an informative, thorough, and entertaining look at the options-trading business through the eyes of a person with a long career as a professional trader, as an individual trader, and as an educator.

After reviewing options basics and explaining a variety of strategies appropriate for nonprofessional traders (Chapters 1 to 4), Dan gives a first-hand account in Chapters 5 and 6 of the mindset of the market maker—the person on the "other side" of the nonprofessional's trade. Nonprofessional traders, or as Dan calls them, *market takers*, can benefit greatly from Dan's insights in many ways. First, nonprofessional traders must understand how they attempt to make money and why that is different from how market makers attempt to make money (Chapters 11, 15, and others). Second, non-professionals must understand why they should not fear market makers, that market makers are *not the enemy* (Chapter 6). Dan shows how market takers and market makers can both prosper from taking opposite sides of the same trade because they use different strategies and have different time frames. Third, nonprofessionals must focus on what is really important in making a trade. Fourth and equally significant, they must know what is not important (Chapter 5).

Dan also makes the dreaded "v word"—*volatility*—accessible. In Chapters 13 and 14 (and earlier in discussions of option price behavior) Dan discusses aspects of volatility—some academic, some practical, but all essential—that every option trader needs to know. Throughout this book Dan cuts through the noise and hype that permeates this industry; he focuses on key concepts and provides a clear message.

Psychology is an important part of trading, and throughout *The Market Taker's Edge* Dan discusses the characteristics that make successful traders. His many stories that relate how he rose through the ranks on the trading floor and share the ups and downs of his trading career help develop the right mindset for trading.

In Chapters 7, 8, and 9, Dan provides much detail about the ever-important tactical matter of entering option orders. He discusses what traders need to know, from their own forecast and their own urgency, to the thinking of the market maker on the other side of the trade. This makes Dan's book a valuable how-to guide for trade execution.

Dan's engaging style and frequently humorous stories make *The Market Taker's Edge* not just an essential book for education but also a pleasure to read. This is a great book for beginners and experienced traders alike. It is both informative and interesting. The *Market Taker's Edge* is on my list of must-read books for option traders.

Jim Bittman
Chicago, Illinois
February 2011

ACKNOWLEDGMENTS

Many people have influenced me throughout my career in the options industry. The readers of this book are the beneficiaries of some of the knowledge that I've gained from them, and the stories created with them.

First and foremost, I'd like to give special thanks to Jim Bittman, who has nurtured my career as a teacher and an author. Thanks also to others in the CBOE's Options Institute, like Debra Peters and Marty Kearney, for helping in my efforts as an options teacher.

Thanks to Bob Kirkland and the late Steve Fossett, who both helped me by giving me my first break as a trader.

Thanks to the team at McGraw-Hill, especially Jennifer Ashkenazy for all the help, support, and opportunity they gave me.

Thanks to my wife Kathleen and children, Sam and Isabel, for their patience and support during the writing of this book.

And mostly, I'd like to thank the trading community in Chicago. Many traders; brokers; clerks; runners; front-office, back-office, and middle-office people; writers; publishers; educators; exchanges (especially the CBOE and CME Group); individuals at the exchanges; and industry executives have helped me along the way since I first stepped on the trading floor in 1993. I've loved being part of this community, and I welcome this opportunity to give back to it.

DISCLAIMER AND DISCLOSURE

This book is both a collection of stories from the author's career in the options industry and an educational guide. The intent of this book is both to entertain the reader and to make the reader more knowledgeable in options and, therefore, more prepared as a self-directed trader. This book is emphatically *not* intended to offer advice.

Many of the assertions in this book represent the author's opinions and personal perspective and should not be construed as fact. This book does not advocate a specific trading system or methodology but instead offers only general education. Best efforts for accuracy have been made, but complete accuracy is not guaranteed.

Any strategies discussed or implied within this book, including examples using actual securities and actual price data, are strictly for illustrative and educational purposes only. They are not to be construed as an endorsement, recommendation, or solicitation to buy or sell any financial instrument. Examples may or may not be based on factual or historical data.

In order to simplify the computations, examples may not include commissions, fees, margin, interest, taxes, or other transaction costs. These types of transaction costs will impact the outcome of all stock, commodity, bond, option, or other financial instrument trades, and they must be considered prior to entering into any transactions. Investors should consult their tax advisor about tax consequences. Past performance does not guarantee future results.

Options involve risk and are not suitable for all investors or traders. Although much of this book focuses on the risks involved in option trading, there are market situations and scenarios that involve unique risks that are not discussed. Prior to buying or selling an option, you should read *Characteristics and Risks of Standardized Options (ODD)*. Copies of the *ODD* are available from your broker, by calling 1-888-OPTIONS, or from the Options Clearing Corporation at One North Wacker Drive, Chicago, Illinois.

INTRODUCTION
My Story

It was raining on LaSalle Street in Chicago. And as any red-blooded ag (i.e., agricultural) trader knows, *rain makes grain*. It was there, that day, that this trader, like many before me, sowed my first seeds in the options business. I never looked back.

It's a common story, really. Just days after graduating college, I put on my best suit (which was also my worst suit, being as it was the only one I owned) and knocked on every door of the Chicago Board of Trade Building. I handed out résumés. I introduced myself. I was looking for a job: clerk, runner, floor sweeper, anything. I just wanted to get onto that trading floor.

I had attended college in Chicago, walking distance from the exchanges. There were many days that I'd spend my downtime between classes sitting in the visitor's gallery of one of the exchange floors watching, learning, and dreaming. Though I didn't yet understand how it all worked, I knew it was where I wanted to be.

As fate would have it, I did, in fact, get my proverbial foot in the door and onto the trading floor. My first job out of college was as a "runner" on the floor of the Chicago Board of Trade (CBOT), which is now part of the CME Group. While my friends who were embarking on their careers were starting out making $30,000 or $40,000 a year at their entry-level jobs, my first situation paid $9,000 a year. And I was about happy as a young man could be.

It wasn't that I wasn't worried about making money. In fact, at that point in my life, I was broke. I had several part-time jobs (waiter, cold caller, flower-shop delivery guy, band manager, just to name a few) to help make rent on the Lincoln Park neighborhood apartment in Chicago my roommate and I affectionately dubbed the "Rough in the Diamond." But all traders must pay for their education one way or another. My way was in forgoing much of an immediate-term, would-be salary to have access to some of the best minds in the trading world. It turned out to be the best money I never spent.

On the trading floor, I was exposed to lots of trading styles, techniques, and philosophies. The floor was home to a well-rounded pool of knowledge. I learned technical analysis from one person, market mechanics from another, and options-trading techniques from yet another. I was in the epicenter of the universe for options trading. Because of my experience on the trading floor, I had an advantage over most people who embark on the journey to become traders. I had access to all the information one could desire, right there in one big room—one very Big Room. This information is passed on through word of mouth from one floor denizen to another. Word of mouth is how all floor traders learn their craft. But the information didn't always flow freely. Knowledge was truly the most precious commodity on the floor.

As a runner, the next logical progression in my career was to become either a phone clerk or an arbitrage clerk ("arb clerk"). In these days (circa 1993), a phone clerk was an integral part of the trading process. Phone clerks took orders from traders over the phone, wrote them on an order form, and either handed the paper order to a runner to physically deliver it to a broker in the pit or flashed them into the pit. Phone clerks were the runners' bosses.

The phone clerk for whom I ran would naturally be the one to train me for the position—his position—which was something he wasn't remotely interested in doing. He kept a tight supply on any information that could contribute to my moving up and onto his turf. Apparently, being a phone clerk was not in the cards for me.

I decided to go the other route and pursue a position as an arb clerk. An arb clerk is someone who stands on the outer rim of the trading pit and communicates market information between the brokers in the pit and the phone clerks. (Note that, ironically, this job has little or nothing to do with actual arbitrage.) Arb clerks communicate via the on-the-floor hand-signal language called "arb" or "arbing." This job would bring me closer to the action. I heard about a broker looking for an arb clerk, and I applied for the job.

To say I applied for the job is kind of a misstatement. The process was somewhat informal. The rules involved in applying for a job on the trading floor, especially in those days, were a little different than for other industries. *Rule Number One*: résumés are not really necessary most of the time. If you hand a résumé (especially one on fancy, textured résumé paper) to a floor trader, the trader or broker interviewing you will look at you as if you have three heads. (Note: this is a bit different for off-floor positions, trading or otherwise.) Bottom line: if you can do the job, you can have it. If not, no piece of paper is going to say otherwise. *Rule Number Two*: no suits. Floor traders simply don't wear them; neither do their clerks. The normal work attire in those days (which, by extension, was interview attire) was a collared golf shirt accessorized with the most ridiculous tie in your closet, preferably slightly threadbare, with a few signs of wear—*it showed that you'd been around the block*. (Note: ties are no longer required on the Chicago trading floors, which promotes the problem of what to do with my Three Stooges tie and the rest of the bunch.) *Rule Number Three*: there are no rules.

When I applied to be an arb clerk, I walked up to the broker and said, "I hear you're looking for an arb clerk." This began the interview process, which consisted of two questions. First, "Do you know how to arb?" This question was followed by my halfhearted response of "yes?" which in turn was followed by his second and final question, "Can you start Monday?" I had no formal training in this area either: there was none. I learned what I could from watching others, and I was thrown to the wolves.

Any other job with this level of responsibility (there could be literally tens of thousands of dollars on the line with any given hand signal flashed to or from the pit) would have consisted of a thorough training program. I naively thought there would be some sort of training provided by the veteran arb clerk also employed by my new boss. On the morning of my first day, I stood down below the top step on which the arb clerks stood, running errands, watching and practicing my hand signals. The lunch hour rolled around and the other arb clerk with whom I worked simply turned to me and said, "OK. You're up. I'm going to lunch." And he left. Like most of my jobs to come in the trading business, this one's training program was that of trial by fire. Fortunately, I passed.

Fast-forward to four years of clerking later, I became a floor trader, or market maker, on the floor of the Chicago Board Options Exchange (CBOE) and had a fairly long, reasonably prosperous career. But my formative years as a clerk left a mark that would shape me forever. Although it's been said that those who can, do, and those who can't, teach, I've found it to be quite the opposite in the trading business.

In my years on the floor, I found that competent traders with confidence in themselves were generally happy to share their knowledge. The hoarders of information tended to be those who had only a limited supply and were afraid the recipients of their knowledge would pass them by. Ultimately, in this business, it is the talent with which the knowledge is put to use that determines success. And while trial by fire is sometimes a good way to learn (there's nothing like having real money on the line), it is often an expensive way to learn as well.

As mentioned, these and other early experiences in my career were part of a formative period in my life. They helped shape the way I would think about trading, learning, and teaching. The otherwise esoteric information from the trading floor has seldom found its way outside the walls of the exchange until now. But there are many people who can benefit from the knowledge of a trading-floor veteran. After having gained so much from the options industry, I've made it my cause to give back. It is my objective to share the knowledge that many of those on the trading floor won't and those who were never on the floor can't, and to help traders avoid the costly mistakes of trying to learn on their own, through the harsh but ubiquitous trail-by-fire method of learning.

The trading floor is a veritable Petri dish for successful traders. Because of geographical, financial, and practical reasons, not all traders can reap the benefits of starting their careers on the floor. And, undoubtedly, the "floor" has become a virtual, rather than a physical, environment. The Big Room no longer exists. Word of mouth and the education process have become disjointed, and often traders still must learn from the proverbial Black and Blue.

The purpose of this book is to bring a treasure trove of trading-floor knowledge to the reader. This book offers lessons from the trading pits from the perspective of a professional trader turned options evangelist for the benefit of both aspiring professional traders and nonprofessional traders alike.

1

MY FIRST YEAR IN THE OPTIONS BUSINESS

*What I Learned and
How I Learned It*

If there is one thing that characterizes the career of a successful trader, it is humility. No one is bigger than the market. No one can predict the future. No one wins every time. The market has a way of humbling the best of us. Confidence, but not arrogance, is the common thread among those who make it in the options game in the long run.

As a trader on the floor of the Chicago Board Options Exchange (CBOE) for many years, I had the opportunity to watch wave after wave of aspiring traders embark on the journey to carve out their careers in the markets. The Designated Primary Market Maker (DPM) in our pit—the Ford pit—and other traders employed clerks to show them the ropes and groom them to trade. As one would imagine, not all of the clerks ended up as traders.

Over time, I developed a knack for being able to tell which clerks would go on to become successful traders and which ones would not. The ones who watched and listened, learned and internalized—who knew only what they knew and assumed no more—were the ones who stood a fighting chance. The know-it-alls, who had the "secret recipe" for success, who always thought they knew where the stock was going—and who always had an excuse for why it didn't go their way when they were wrong—were the ones destined for an early departure from their careers in options.

There was one particular clerk in my pit who would frequently engage me in conversations always beginning with something like, "Hey PAS (on the CBOE floor, PAS was my acronym that was displayed on my badge), you have to buy these so-and-so calls. Look at this chart; this stock is going up! You can't lose! Blah, blah, blah . . ." This poor young man never made it onto a seat. He never gave himself the chance. Mastery of the options game is about learning to exploit the nuances of a game of chance, *not* predicting the future. This poor sap never appreciated the statistical nature inherent in option trading and never bothered to try to learn.

Followed by humility, another one of the top attributes among successful traders is a lust for learning. The market is dynamic. Winning trading systems have a way to—as the saying goes—*work until they don't work*. Then, when the goose stops laying the proverbial golden eggs, the trader needs to recalibrate, learn from his or her mistakes, adjust to the new market conditions, and start anew. As an author and lecturer, I am still a student of the market. I have been since the onset of my career and always will be.

Every story has a beginning. The tale of my career in the options game is no different. The beginning of this story, like others, sets the stage for the trials and tribulations that unfold later. So, before delving into the complexities of options, let's first examine some basics.

OPTION BASICS: RUDIMENTARY EXPLANATION

Traders who are just starting out in options tend to start with the rudimentary building blocks to gain an academic understanding. To that point, let's begin with the basics of an option contract's inner workings.

Options are contracts between two parties: a buyer and a seller. There are two types of conventional option contracts: calls and puts.

- A *call* is the right, but not the obligation, to buy an underlying asset at a fixed price, called the "strike price," within a given time constraint set by the expiration date.
- A *put* is the right, but not the obligation, to sell an underlying security at a fixed price, also called the "strike price," within a given time constraint set by the expiration date.

The rights extended in these contracts can be bought or sold. A trader who buys an option creates a long (ownership) position in the contract. A trader who sells (writes) an option creates a short (obligatory) position. Buyers of options have the rights stated previously, which they can exercise at their will. Sellers must perform their obligations at the discretion of an option owner (holder) who exercises. When options owners *exercise* their right to buy or sell the underlying asset, sellers who are short an option will, in turn, be *assigned* and therefore be called upon to fulfill their obligation.

Long contracts can be sold to close (ending the right) before their expiration date. Short options can be bought to close (ending the obligation) before the expiration date. So, expiration of the contract or exercise or assignment may not occur.

ALTERNATIVE BEGINNINGS

As mentioned, every story has a beginning. But the standard, academic explanation of options stated here is not the only way to begin this saga. In fact, it is not at all how my foray into options began. As discussed in the introduction of this book, I began my career—and therefore my options education—on the floor of the Chicago exchanges. I am truly fortunate to have started in the business in such a manner, as it is surely the best way to achieve a mastery of options, in my humble opinion. But, for all its advantages, during my rearing as a budding trader, the prevalent trial-by-fire education method proved to be nonnurturing—to say the least.

Many of the educational options courses of which I have been a part since working with *stay-at-home traders** spend hours on the rights-and-obligations discussion stated previously. This circumstantial minutia was merely assumed knowledge for any new entrant on the trading floor in my early days as a student of the market. Aspiring traders clerking on the floor, striving to master the art of trading, would move forth with a rapid trajectory, soaking in knowledge through every pore.

The chronology of concepts absorbed on the floor is mere chicken-versus-egg trivia. From day one on the trading floor, I was submersed in options lingo, culture, and trading activity during the workday. I—and my ambitious fellow traders-in-training who were hungry for an opportunity to conquer the pits—would eat, drink, and sleep options after leaving the confines of the walls of the exchange, reading books, reviewing the day's activities, and preparing for the next trading day.

Clerks first needed to gain enough knowledge to perform the duties required to assist the trader for whom they worked. If a clerk couldn't do his job, he was fired. Knowing just enough afforded the clerk the opportunity to keep his or her job. But knowing enough to keep your job, however, required a fair amount of knowledge, some of which was what would be considered that of an advanced nature. Any precursory information not relevant to the task at hand could be easily "backfilled." And it could be learned at a later time. *You have to know what you have to know.*

For example, traders would often ask their clerks for their profit and loss, or P&L, on a particular trade. To an options market maker, the nature of this question was that of *theoretical profit* (more on that later), which required some math and knowledge of option metrics and pricing to answer. At its simplest level, it is a comparison of the trade price to the theoretical value that is generated by the trader's pricing model—a fairly simple arithmetic calculation. The answer to the question might be something like, say, 6 cents per contract on,

---

*The author prefers not to use the generally accepted industry term "retail traders" to describe traders who trade from home in an online brokerage account. The word *retail*, however, can have negative connotations. So, the phrase "stay-at-home traders" is occasionally used instead of "retail traders" throughout this book.

maybe, 100 contracts. The simple reply that would satisfy the trader's question would be "6 cents." In fact, on a busy day, a more detailed answer would likely result in the clerk getting chewed out for the distraction. *Six cents*; that's it.

But, in the equity options world, 6 cents isn't 6 cents. It's $6. And on a hundred lot, it's $600. Studious clerks would need to very quickly get a crash course in contract specifications to intellectualize the translation of pennies to dollars by learning the contract specifications.

EQUITY OPTION CONTRACT SPECIFICATIONS

Equity options listed on an exchange are standardized for the purpose of being fungible—therefore enabling liquid trading with a seamless exchange of options of the same series. Each standard U.S.-listed equity option (call or put) represents the rights to either buy or sell, respectively, 100 shares of the underlying stock. Therefore, a trader who owns one call option may exercise it to acquire 100 shares of stock. A trader who owns one put option may exercise to sell, or sell short, 100 shares. Specifically, the contract offers the right to trade the stock at a fixed price, called the "strike price"—a right that lasts until the expiration date of the option.

Example
The following is an example of a typical equity option contract.

Buy one DIS October 32 call at 1.40.

Strike Price
In this example, 32 is the strike price, that is, the price at which the shares will be purchased should the trader choose to exercise the call. The trader is buying one call option, therefore giving him the right to buy 100 shares of the Walt Disney Company (DIS) at $32 a share.

Expiration Date
Because the DIS equity option, like any equity option listed in the United States, is an American-style exercise option, the call may be

exercised at any time the option is in the trader's inventory starting on the date the trader takes possession of the option and ending on either the expiration date or the date when the option is
sold. This is different from a European-style option, which may
only be exercised at expiration. The expiration date is generally the
Saturday following the third Friday of the stated month. So, in this
Disney (DIS) example, expiration comes on the Saturday following
the third Friday of October. Up until the expiration date, the call
may be exercised as long as it is in the trader's inventory. If the
trader sells the option (thereby taking a profit or loss on the
contract itself) before the expiration date, the right to exercise is
forgone.

Moneyness
The DIS equity option—like any other—would only be exercised if
it is to the option holder's advantage to do so. Remember: *right, not
obligation*. Therefore, an option would only be exercised under a certain set of circumstances. For one, an option would usually only be
exercised if it is *in-the-money*.

In-the-money calls have intrinsic value. When they are exercised, the underlying stock is bought below the current stock price.
Thus the call must be worth at least the difference between the
strike price and the higher stock price. In-the-money puts have a
strike price above the current stock price. They intrinsically must
be worth the difference between the strike price and the lower
stock price.

The opposite state to in-the-money is *out-of-the-money*. Out-of-
the-money options have no intrinsic value, and therefore they usually provide no incentive to exercise. Why would a trader want to
buy above the current market price or sell below it?* Out-of-the-
money calls have strike prices above the current market value.
Out-of-the-money puts have strike prices below the current market
value.

---

*There may in fact be situations in which a trader may decide to exercise by excep-
tion an out-of-the-money option, or forgo exercising an in-the-money option. More
on this later.

Finally, *at-the-money options*, for both calls and puts, have strike prices that are equal to the current stock price. It is common practice to refer to the nearest strike price to the current stock price as the at-the-money strike. Sometimes, this is called a *near-the-money option*.

Please note, the state of moneyness—in-the-money, at-the-money, or out-of-the-money—is merely a description of the proximity of stock price to strike price. It is *not* indicative of whether or not the trade is profitable. For example, an in-the-money option can be bought and then later sold for either a profit or a loss. So can out-of-the-money or at-the-money options, for that matter.

Option Premium

Certainly the right afforded in an option contract has value. Who wouldn't want the prerogative, without being obligated, to buy (or sell) a stock at a fixed price? This right can only benefit a trader. Therefore, there is a price, also called a premium, associated with each option. For the right inherent in the DIS call, the trader is paying a premium of $1.40, or $140 per call contract.

Because owning the right in and of itself can only be a benefit, options cannot trade for less than zero. In addition to the in-the-money value of an option (also called "intrinsic value" or "parity value"), an option can have time value. Specifically, time value is any option value over parity. Moneyness, time to expiration, volatility, interest, and expected dividends all affect the time value of an option.

OTHER OPTIONABLE ASSETS

There are many assets other than equities on which options are listed. For securities, there are options on indexes, exchange-traded funds (ETFs), HOLDRs, and more. For commodities, options are listed on many tangible and intangible assets categorized by metals, softs, grains, Treasuries, stocks, energy, and more.

Some index securities options, for example, SPX—an index options contract that represents the Standard & Poor's (S&P) 500

Index—are cash-settled, European-style exercise. *Cash settled* means that when an option is exercised, the exerciser receives the in-the-money value of the option instead of physical shares; the short-option trader who is assigned pays the in-the-money value. Further, *European-style options* can only be exercised at expiration, not before, as American exercise allows.

Commodity options typically expire into futures. For example, if one corn call option is exercised, the trader would buy one corn future at the strike price. The contract specifications for futures options can be very different from securities options. For example, in both equity and ETF options, 1 penny equals $1 (because, again, each option is stated on a per-share basis and represents the rights on 100 shares). In corn or soybeans, however, 1 penny equals $50 (because each contract is stated per bushel and represents the rights on 5,000 bushels).

Listed securities options are overseen by the U.S. Securities and Exchange Commission (SEC). Exchange-traded commodities options are overseen by the U.S. Commodity Futures Trading Commission (CFTC). There is also another forum for option trading of both securities and commodity options called the "over-the-counter (OTC) market." OTC options are not listed on an exchange. They are contracts that are more customizable than the standard-ized listed options facilitated by an exchange.

The OTC market is a significant part of the panoptic options market. However, OTC trades are not usually observable by anyone other than professional traders. The trade size with OTC option trades tends to be very big, because the OTC market is typically traded only by well-capitalized professionals. Another way it differs from other options markets is with clearing.

CLEARING

Options are big business. Just in the listed options arena alone, more than $1 billon in option premiums commonly changes hands each day. On some days, there can be big winners and big losers, especially among large institutional traders. The question arises: what happens in the case of default?

Each trader of listed options has a clearing firm—which guarantees each trade on behalf of the trader. For nonprofessionals, brokers represent the trades to the clearing firms. Professionals are housed directly with a clearing firm. Each clearing firm guarantees performance on every contract traded by traders who clear through that firm.

Each individual clearing firm is, in turn, guaranteed by the central clearing house. For listed securities options, options are cleared through the Options Clearing Corporation (OCC). The OCC clears all listed options traded on the eight U.S. options exchanges. There are a handful of central clearing firms for commodity options, the largest being CME Group Clearing.

LIAISONS OF INFORMATION

While a small group of floor-trading firms had structured, intensive trader training programs in my early days on the floor, most did not. Still, clerks were satiated with the sensibilities of the trader mentality. They were inundated with enlightenment as they worked as conduits of information between the trader for whom they were employed and all the terminals of market data needed to facilitate trading.

Clerks would need to verify trades with brokers and rectify trades with clearing firms. They'd need to know when the "numbers" were—that is, when government announcements, earnings, and other anticipated economic events were scheduled to take place. They'd need to verify positions, option-trading metrics, and trade prices. And they had to be right.

There is a reputation among floor traders that, in my opinion, is reasonably accurate: *floor traders are intense*. Traders need to be loud and boisterous to be heard in open outcry. Though it is largely unacceptable in many work environments, shouting is a normal means of communication on the trading floor. Yet, I did know a few traders who were as docile as kittens—just not many.

Clerks who worked for the few particularly intense traders on the trading floor *really* needed to be right, not just to avoid making a mistake that could cost their trader money but to prevent the aftermath that would follow: *the public humiliation of being berated in front of the entire pit.* Avoiding this fate was a big motivator for many clerks. The sometimes tough work environment truly did build character and confidence among many budding traders, present company included. As Friedrich Nietzsche said, "That which doesn't kill me makes me stronger."

MARKET DATA

Clerks would necessarily learn to think like a trader. They'd learn to have the answer before a question was asked. And they'd know where to find the answers. Many could be found by a search on a nearby computer placed in the pit by the exchange for member access. Other information would need to be verbally communicated by a phone clerk or other trading-floor personnel or back-office people. Any vigilant clerk would keep a list of phone numbers in his jacket pocket for such occasions. Some data came from the exchange itself. Much of the information needed was market data.

The Market

The term *market*, in its purest sense, is the stated bid and offer on a specific asset. The *bid* is the highest price any market participant will pay for the asset. The *offer* (or *ask price*) is the lowest price at which any market participant will sell it. For example, say the market for the DIS October 32 call is 1.35 bid, offered at 1.40. This would mean the highest price anyone in the world (at this very moment in time) will pay for this call is 1.35 per contract. The lowest price anyone will sell it for is 1.40 per contract. There may be more than one person "on the bid" or "on the offer" also hoping to buy or sell, respectively, at those prices.

In this example, the market is 1.35–1.40. In professional trading environments, this would be orated, "one thirty-five bid, at one forty" or simply, "one thirty-five, at forty" or just "thirty-five, forty." Again, the fewer words spoken to explain the market, the better. The bid is always stated first, then the offer, which is sometimes preceded by the word *at*. The handle—or, the number(s) before the decimal in equity options—is generally assumed and usually disregarded whenever possible. The reason? If a trader is so far off the market that he or she doesn't know what the handle is, that trader shouldn't be in the pit.

The market is "made" by a certain kind of trader, called a "market maker." Market makers make a living by buying the bid and selling the offer in hopes of locking in a profit (more on this later). In a given physical trading pit, there may be between one and a few hundred market makers.

A specific type of clerk, called an arb clerk (my second job on the trading floor), is a liaison of market information with regard to the underlying asset. This clerk relays information between an options market maker and a broker in that underlying instrument. Market makers trade the underlying as a hedge and must always know exactly where the market for the underlying is trading. This information is still, to this day, communicated via hand signals in many of the remaining trading pits. Traders' assistants would also sometimes need to get markets in other instruments. Accurate and timely—timely, as in *at this exact moment in time*—market information is essential to market makers.

Time and Sales

One bit of information that is often needed by traders is *time and sales*. Time and sales is the definitive record of all bids, offers, and trades that have been made during a trading day with corresponding times. If there is a question about a trade that occurred as to whether the price has been reasonable or within the confines of the bid-ask spread at the time, time and sales will tell.

Volume and Open Interest

Trades are consummated by a buyer and a seller both agreeing on a price, thereby entering into a contract, hence executing a trade with each other. When a contract is created, *open interest* increases. Open interest is the running total of the number of contracts in existence for a specific option series. When a contract is closed, open interest decreases for that series. Open interest is often studied in conjunction with volume.

Volume is the number of contracts traded (whether opened or closed) in a single trading day. Volume begins at zero at the beginning of each trading day.

THE LITTLE DETAILS AND THE BIG PICTURE

My first year on the trading floor seemed to be full of a million little nuggets of information like this, not all of which could possibly fit in a single chapter. The details were great in number. But there were also a few big-picture ideas learned that year, specifically as to the psychology of what it takes to make it as a trader.

People who work on the trading floor commonly change jobs, sometimes frequently. This is especially true for ambitious people when they are first starting out. In my first year, I went on several job interviews and held a total of four or five jobs. As mentioned in the introduction to this book, many of the entry-level job interviews were very short and to the point—*Can you do the job? OK, can you start Monday?* But those aimed at becoming a trader's assistant— someone who would need to think like a trader, and one day perhaps become a trader—were a bit more involved. Yet, they were surprisingly even more unconventional.

For instance, I was on one job interview. It started out, as one might expect, with questions such as, "Who was your previous employer?" and, "What were your responsibilities?" Then the line of questioning changed to the likes of, "If you had a stack of quarters that went from the street level up to the top of the Sears Tower, could you fit them all in your closet?"* The questions of this nature were accompanied by piercing eye contact and an impatient attitude from the interviewer.

The intent of this (fairly common) interrogation routine was to ascertain certain things about the interviewee, all of which related to important traits necessary for someone to make it as a trader. *Can*

---

*The answer to the question about the Sears Tower and the quarters is fairly simple. Yes, the quarters could easily fit in a typical closet. With the great skyscraper reaching 110 stories tall, one could divide the huge stack of quarters into 110 stacks, one story tall each, arranged side-by-side, 10 rows by 11 rows.

this individual think outside the box? The market doesn't always act rationally. Surprising events happen in the market all of the time. Traders need to be able to use logic and figure things out. *Can this person perform under pressure?* With real money on the line—sometimes a lot—and in fast-moving markets, traders need to perform well under pressure. And, *can this person think abstractly?* Abstract thought is supremely necessary for an option trader, specifically in relation to the volatility component of option trading.

2

THE DIFFERENCE BETWEEN ME AND YOU

When I started on the floor of the Chicago Board Options Exchange, options traded in "teenies," or sixteenths of a dollar. Both stocks and options traded in fractions, unlike the decimal trading to which traders are accustomed today. Stocks were permitted to trade in a tick size as low as one-eighth of a dollar (12.5 cents). Options could trade in a minimum tick size of one-sixteenth of a dollar (6.25 cents). Traders, essentially, have their own dialect as trading floor lingo has evolved over time. This vernacular has arisen generally for the purpose of shortening words and phrases to share information more quickly and efficiently. Hence, the bastardization of a sixteenth became a teenie (also sometimes called a "stinth").

One day, early in my trading career as a market maker, a new, young trader began trading in the pit in which I traded. There was usually a breaking-in period for each trader as the members of the trading pit adjust to having a new member in the crowd. As in any social environment, assimilation was a slow process. But in the case of the trading floor, it was, perhaps, a bit more difficult to gain acceptance, as all the members of the pit were in direct competition with one another.

One day, a dispute arose between the new trader and one of the old-guard members of the pit. The dispute was over a teenie—$6.25 on a one-lot option contract. The tiff went on for a bit as the two headstrong competitors battled for what amounted to less than a day's lunch money. As the dispute came to its climax, the new trader finally said, "It's a teenie. What's the big deal? What's a teenie?" To this, the veteran trader responded, "What's a teenie? It's the difference between where I live and where you live."

THE WINNERS AND THE LOSERS

The statement of the long-time pit trader profoundly illustrates the objective of any successful trader. Professional traders, market makers in particular, who have longevity in the markets strive to earn a small, modest profit on each contract traded and likewise trade a large number of contracts to make up for the meager profits in volume. *Pennies add up.* A market maker who can grind out a few cents per contract can have a robust, sustainable business that can be very financially rewarding. Everyone likes a home-run trade. But in trading, being a piggy (too greedy a trader) is not a sustainable business model.

This philosophy is true for retail traders as well. As the trading idiom goes: *pigs get slaughtered.* To make money as a trader, the goal is to have consistency. It is not about having one single trade that leads to riches. I've actually met an aspiring retail trader who told me he wanted to learn to trade so he could make enough money so that he didn't have to trade anymore. That is a lousy goal. Passion begets success. To be good at anything, professionals need to love what they do. Otherwise, why bother? Go try to make money at what you love. You'll likely be more successful.

Success in trading is about having made a great return at the end of the year. This is true whether the traders are professional or

retail. There is, however, a difference between retail and professional traders in the methodology in attaining results.

PROFESSIONAL TRADERS VS. RETAIL TRADERS

Professional traders and retail traders trade differently from each
other. Retail traders are necessarily more inclined to position-trade
than are professional traders such as market makers. Market makers, effectively, profit by buying the bid and selling the offer; something that non–market makers cannot do except in rare occasions.
Therefore, retail traders must trade by taking a position on each
trade, which requires (1) being somewhat good at forecasting and
(2) having skill in both crafting and managing trades. Further, the
commission structure, slippage, and margin requirements faced by
retail traders usually prohibit them from trading the tiny-profit-per-
contract strategies that a floor trader can trade.

Retail traders can't strive to make a few cents per trade if their
commissions can be more than a few cents per contract. One dollar
per contract of commission is equal to 1 cent of option premium.
(Remember, options are priced on a per-share basis, and a typical
equity option represents 100 shares. Hence, 1 cent of option premium equals $1 of actual cash.) When there are ticket charges
involved (or a per-trade commission, as opposed to a per-contract
commission), the commissions can significantly cut into profits,
especially those of one-lot and two-lot traders.

Also, unlike market makers who buy the bid and sell the offer,
retail (and institutional) traders buy the (higher) offer price and sell
the (lower) bid. This less tangible transaction cost is called "slippage." The bid-ask spread for a somewhat liquid option contract is
typically about 2 to 5 cents, on average. That means that non-market-
maker traders—or "market takers"—need to make several cents on
each trade, as well as cover commissions, just to break even.

Most retail traders are subject to Regulation T (Reg-T) margin
requirements. Reg-T margin is the longstanding system for margin
requirement for retail traders. It dictates how much margin the
Options Clearing Corporation requires a trader to have to initiate a
trade. Most retail traders are subject to Reg-T margining. Margin

requirements are much more restrictive for the typical retail trader trading under Reg-T margining than they are for their professional trading counterparts. Because market makers are integral in providing liquidity to the market and are assumed to be knowledgeable about option risk, they are given a lot of leeway in the form of leverage. Usually, market makers are required to put up only a fraction of the margin a retail trader, trading in a retail account, must put up.

Retail portfolio margining has somewhat narrowed the gap between retail traders and professional traders, in terms of marginability. Retail portfolio margining is similar to market-maker margining, but it doesn't allow for quite so much leverage. It is much less restrictive than Reg-T margining. The relatively new phenomenon of retail portfolio margining has been a huge step forward in leveling the playing field and giving retail traders the ability to trade more kinds of strategies that were otherwise margin-prohibitive. But it also gives traders more than enough rope to hang themselves and should, therefore, only be used by experienced traders. Still, market makers are afforded some margin advantage for their role in facilitating liquidity.

The apparent advantages of market makers come at a cost and would surely be a disadvantage to some wanton traders lusting after these perks. For example, market makers must pay for trading privileges. They must own or lease these privileges, which are sometimes referred to as their "seat." Trading privileges are expensive. At one point, my seat lease was more than $10,000 a month to trade on the CBOE. For most retail traders, paying commission to their online broker is much less oppressive.

Market makers also must pay exchange fees, clearing fees, data fees, office space, clerk salaries, and other charges. Furthermore, they are, under some circumstances, *required* to trade and provide liquidity. Market makers have their own set of trading challenges that are much different from those of nonliquidity providers. Again, market makers don't seek out and actively take positions. They react to order flow. When the rest of the market is buying, it is the market makers who are selling to them; when the market is selling, market makers are buying. Market makers can end up with positions contrary to their forecast and to the conventional wisdom of the market. That can make position management a struggle.

THE ANALYSIS ADVANTAGE

All traders, professional and otherwise, have hurdles to success. To succeed, one must overcome the obstacles inherent in his or her plight. It is how one deals with adversity that leads to success or failure.

For example, sometimes position-trading retail traders reach too far for profits as a result of taking on too much risk and improperly analyzing their positions. Part of the problem for many retail traders is their approach in analyzing potential trades and, subsequently, trades in their inventory. The approach of many nonprofessional traders is rather straightforward and, frankly, oversimplified.

Using the right analyses is one way professional traders and savvy nonprofessionals can truly have an advantage. Professional traders focus on the complete, multifaceted set of option-centric risks. Many retail traders tend to focus only on the fact that calls gain value when the underlying instrument rises and puts gain value when the underlying falls (i.e., direction). Clever traders, however, exploit all option-centric exposure—especially volatility.

TWO APPROACHES TO OPTION RISK MANAGEMENT

In the option trader's nomenclature, risk management means managing the uncertainty of future price changes. Unlike the lay definition of the word *risk*, which focuses solely on loss, in the context of risk management *risk* can mean the possibility of either *profit* or *loss*. Ultimately, risk management is the practice of maximizing profit potential and minimizing potential losses.

There are two different approaches to option risk management. One can observe risk from the perspective of *absolute risk*—the maximum profit or loss achieved once all time value has left the option. Or risk can be studied in terms of *incremental risk*—the risk resulting from incremental changes in the pricing factors affecting an option.

ABSOLUTE RISK

Let's start with two basic principles to understanding absolute risk. The following two points are mantras taught to every new option trader:

- Long options have limited loss and unlimited profit potential.
- Short options have limited profit potential and unlimited loss.

These phrases are helpful memory devices designed to give traders a baseline from which to start. However, technically, these axioms are true only for calls. Stocks can rise indefinitely. Therefore, long calls can profit indefinitely, and short calls can lose indefinitely.

But the profit potential of long puts and loss potential for short puts are actually limited. A long put will become more profitable as the price of the underlying instrument declines. The prices of stocks, commodities, indexes, ETFs, and other trading instruments, however, can only fall to zero. Therefore, profits on the long put are limited. The same logic applies to short puts, which lose as the underlying falls: losses on short puts are limited by the asset falling to zero. Despite their technical shortcomings, the previous points are still worthy of committing to memory. To be sure, a trader who is short a put and watches the underlying stock fall to zero will certainly *feel* as if the position has unlimited risk, as it will be a costly trade that—with 20-20 hindsight—would likely not be worth the risk reward.

A full appreciation of absolute risk of an option position requires a more precise analysis than the discussion has provided thus far. Option values may consist of two parts: *time value* and *intrinsic value*. By definition, only in-the-money options have intrinsic value. Any part of an option premium that is not intrinsic value is referred to as "time value." The time value portion of an option premium has value mostly because of the uncertainty of the future price action of the underlying asset (i.e., volatility). When an option expires, it no longer contains any time value. At that point, the option is either worth its intrinsic value or worth zero.

Determination of the absolute risk of an option is rather straightforward. With no time left in the life of the option and, hence, no possibility for future volatility within its lifespan, the only pricing variable is the price of the underlying instrument at the exact point in time of expiration. The price of the underlying asset determines whether the option is at-the-money or out-of-the-money—and consequently worth zero—or in-the-money, and thus worth its intrinsic value.

The relationship of profitability relative to the price of the underlying asset at expiration can be expressed in a graph. This is commonly represented by an at-expiration profit-and-loss diagram, commonly referred to as an "at-expiration diagram" or a "P&L diagram."

At-Expiration Diagrams

An at-expiration diagram is a two-dimensional diagram, with the y axis (the vertical axis) representing the profit or loss on the option position, and the x axis (the horizontal axis) representing the price of the underlying asset at expiration. The absolute risk of any option strategy consisting entirely of options with the same expiration date can be expressed by an at-expiration diagram.*

For the purpose of illustrating absolute risk in P&L diagrams, let's look at the four basic option positions: long call, long put, short call, and short put. First, let's examine the long call. As mentioned, long options have limited loss and unlimited profit potential. If the call is at-the-money or out-of-the-money at expiration, it is worth zero, and the loss is equal to the entire premium paid. If the long call is in-the-money at expiration, it is worth its intrinsic value and will profit or lose as if it were a long stock position. (It would, in fact, become a long position if it were held until expiration. Equity options in-the-money by more than $0.01 as of the underlying instrument's closing price on the last trading day before expiration are automatically exercised by the OCC unless directed to the contrary by the option owner.)

---

*Strategies containing options with differing expiration dates (e.g., calendar spreads) can only be estimated with an at-expiration diagram.

Example: Long Call

Imagine a trader makes the following trade in the iShares Russell 2000 Index Fund (IWM) and holds it until expiration:

Buy one IWM March 65 call at 2.30.

Figure 2.1 shows the profit or loss on the call, given the price of IWM at expiration. This diagram shows that if IWM is trading at or below $65 a share at expiration, the loss on the call is limited to 2.30, or the entire premium paid. If IWM is above $65 at expiration, the call is worth its intrinsic value. The higher the price of the ETF, the greater the call profits. The price of IWM can, theoretically, rise to infinity; thus can the price of the call.

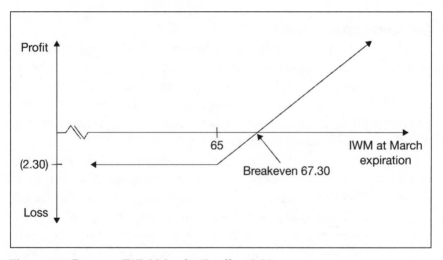

Figure 2.1 Buy one IWM March 65 call at 2.30.

Figure 2.1 also pinpoints the exact price at which the trade becomes profitable (at expiration)—the *breakeven point*. The only way the call can have value at expiration is if it has intrinsic value. Because the price paid for the call initially was 2.30, the intrinsic value must be greater than 2.30 in order to reap a profit. Therefore, if IWM is above $67.30 (meaning the 65-strike call has more than 2.30 of intrinsic value), the call is profitable. If IWM is below $67.30 (at which point the 65-strike call would have less than 2.30 of intrinsic value), the trade is a loser.

Another way to think of the breakeven point is in terms of exercise mechanics. If the call is in-the-money at expiration it, essentially, becomes a long position of 100 shares of IWM purchased at its strike price, $65. But the premium paid, 2.30, is an expense and must also be considered. Therefore, the effective purchase price of the shares would be $67.30. If IWM is below $67.30, the trade is a loser. Above that breakeven point the trade is a winner, with increasing profits for each tick higher in the underlying.

Example: Long Put

The absolute risk of a long put can be visualized just as easily with an at-expiration diagram. But with the put, the risk of loss is to the upside and profit is to the downside.

Imagine a trader buys the following put in General Electric Company (GE) and holds it until expiration:

Buy one GE January 16 put at 1.10.

Figure 2.2 shows the profit or loss on the put, given the price of GE stock at expiration.

If GE is above the strike price of $16 a share at expiration, the put that was purchased at 1.10 will expire and the premium paid will represent a loss in its entirety. If, however, GE shares are trading below $16 at expiration, the put will be in-the-money and be

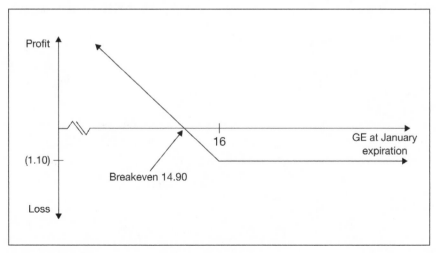

Figure 2.2 Buy one GE January 16 put at 1.10.

worth its intrinsic value. To show a profit, GE must be trading with a high enough intrinsic value to cover the initial cost of the trade. Here, the breakeven point is $14.90 (the strike price *minus* the premium paid).

The farther below $14.90, the greater the profit. Profits are capped at $14.90 because stocks cannot trade below zero. At $0 the 16 put would have $16 worth of intrinsic value. The $16 in intrinsic value minus the $1.10 premium paid yields a maximum potential profit of $14.90. Again, this is if GE stock were to drop all the way to zero before the option expires.

Example: Short Call

Short calls have limited profit potential and unlimited loss potential. Many retail brokers restrict the majority of their traders from selling calls outright (i.e., not "covered" by a long stock position and not part of a spread). Most professionals avoid selling calls outright because the risks seldom justify the reward.

The trader in this example makes this trade in Apple Inc. (AAPL) calls:

Sell one AAPL September 270 call at 12.00.

Figure 2.3 shows the profit or loss on the call, given the price of AAPL shares at expiration. Here, the profit is limited to the 12.00

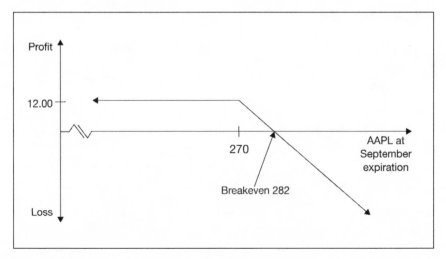

Figure 2.3 Sell one AAPL September 270 call at 12.00.

premium initially received, which is enjoyed if AAPL stock is below $270 at September expiration. However, if the stock is above the strike price at expiration, the call will trade at parity, acting like short stock. Because equities have no upward bounds, possible losses are unlimited. The breakeven point is established where the 270 call has $12 of intrinsic value, or $282.

Example: Short Put

Short puts are often thought of as low-risk strategies by people who consider themselves to be conservative investors. In fact, from a trading risk management perspective, short puts have fairly high risk in comparison to similar alternatives, as they have significant loss potential relative to limited potential gains.

In this example, a trader will sell the following put in Nordstrom, Inc. (JWN):

Sell one JWN December 36 put at 3.20.

Figure 2.4 shows the profit or loss on the put, given the price of JWN shares at expiration.

On this limited-profit position, the maximum reward is set at 3.20, the premium collected, which is enjoyed if JWN is above the $36 strike price at expiration. If JWN is below the strike at expiration, the put would be worth parity, acting like long stock (which,

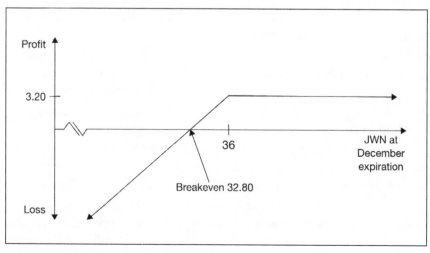

Figure 2.4 Sell one JWN December 36 put at 3.20.

of course, it would likely become as a result of assignment, if it were held to expiration). The breakeven point here is $32.80.

If this put is indeed assigned, resulting in a long stock position, the effective purchase price of the stock is, likewise, $32.80. The long shares would be actually bought at the strike price of $36, but the credit received is taken into consideration. Therefore, the maximum risk is $32.80, which would be suffered in the highly unlikely event that the stock price would fall to zero.

Benefits and Shortcomings of Absolute Risk

Absolute risk must be known on every trade. Newer traders should make a habit of drawing out at-expiration diagrams. (Don't cheat and let your online broker do it for you!) Experienced traders can calculate the relevant points (i.e., maximum profit, maximum loss, and breakeven) in their head. In fact, that may be the only way some professional traders can ascertain absolute risk.

A while ago, I was interviewing candidates for a job to work as options instructors. One of the criteria for candidacy dictated that the applicant be a current or former professional trader. Upon arrival at the job interview, traders were given a test that included a few questions that required them to draw at-expiration diagrams for various option strategies. Unexpectedly, more than a fair share of market makers couldn't complete that part of the test!

This rather interesting observation in some ways spotlights the shortcoming of at-expiration P&L diagrams. Why couldn't many of the market makers draw these simple diagrams? They are not in the habit of doing so: *they don't need to do so*. These visual aids reflect position risk only at the exact moment of expiration. Market makers, "upstairs traders," and, undoubtedly, most stay-at-home traders don't hold options until expiration. But does that render the study of absolute risk useless? Not necessarily.

Absolute risk is the P&L that the position is moving toward as time passes and the volatility portion (or, time value portion) of the option premium gets less and less relevant. Expiration aside, options may also trade with no time value if they are very deep in-the-money or very far out-of-the-money (at which point they would be zero). That makes knowledge of absolute risk relevant prior to expiration—but only if there is a very dynamic move in the underlying asset. The absolutes illustrated on P&L diagrams are maximum thresholds of profit or loss at expiration and, sometimes, even before.

INCREMENTAL RISK

Though absolute risk must be known, it is incremental risk that is truly of more use to traders on a day-to-day basis. There are only a few influences on the value of an option, each of which have independent incremental effects. In the now-famous paper, "The Pricing of Options and Corporate Liabilities," published in the *Journal of Political Economy* in 1973, Fisher Black and Myron Scholes distilled the risks of options down to but a handful of factors. Moneyness, time, interest, dividends, and volatility are the finite set of risks with which a trader must be concerned.

The factors of interest and dividends are encapsulated in the concept of the time value of money. Incremental changes may occur in both the expectations for and the actual changes of interest rates and future dividend streams, and they affect option value. The other three aforementioned pricing factors (moneyness, time, and the volatility component of option pricing) have a single commonality that binds them together as the major justification for option value: *the uncertainty of the future price of the underlying asset within the life of the contract.*

The right to buy (in the case of a call) or sell (in the case of a put) at a set price has value because of assumptions about future volatility. Because options are a right that needn't be exercised, volatility can only be beneficial to an option owner—at expiration, the option either can be worth zero or have positive value associated with it. Therefore, this right has a monetary value associated with it.

The value of the volatility portion of an option's price (again, also called "time value") is at the heart of option trading. Novice traders, however, commonly overlook volatility. The understanding and subsequent use of volatility is the great divide that separates clever traders from the marks destined for a short career in option trading. Fortunately, volatility is relatively easy to observe.

Figure 2.5 shows two different points in time of the same long-call position. The solid line represents the call's profit or loss at expiration; the dashed line shows the estimated profit or loss at some moment in time *prior* to expiration. For all intents and purposes, the dashed line represents volatility; specifically, it represents implied volatility.

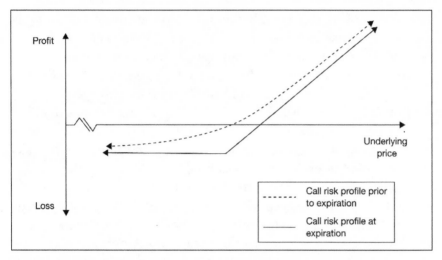

Figure 2.5 Two different chronological points in the same long-call position.

Realized Volatility and Implied Volatility

Though volatility is of the utmost importance to option trading, it is often misunderstood. Some of this misunderstanding stems from the multiple contexts of the word *volatility* used in option trading.

Realized Volatility

The actual volatility of price movements in the underlying asset plays an integral role in option pricing. Again, the more volatility in the underlying instrument, the more opportunity that option holders have to make a profit (or suffer a loss). To be useful as analytical data, the volatility of the underlying must be quantified. In the context of option trading, the price volatility experienced by the underlying is measured by realized, sometimes called historical, volatility.

Realized volatility is stated in terms of a standard deviation observed over a recent time period and is then annualized. Typically, daily closing prices of the asset being traded are used as occurrences in the standard deviation calculation.

Definition: Realized volatility is the annualized standard deviation of daily returns.

Implied Volatility

It follows that when realized volatility is high, options would be dearer, and that when realized volatility is low, options will be cheaper. Considering that options can be used as a hedge, they are a veritable insurance policy. As with other types of insurance policies, when there is greater risk of loss, premiums rise. Further, when expectations about future realized volatility changes, option values can change to reflect altered expectations (all other pricing factors held constant). This embedded volatility pricing component within an options value is called "implied volatility."

Definition: Implied volatility is the volatility component of an option's value.

Like realized volatility, implied volatility is stated in terms of annualized standard deviation. Implied volatility is often thought of as the (collective) market's expectations about the future realized volatility of an asset between the present moment and expiration that is implied by its option price.

Volatility and Incremental Risk

Figure 2.5 in this chapter is telling as it shows much more than initially meets the eye. It is a graphic representation of the three option-centric risks rooted in volatility—implied volatility, time, and moneyness.

P&L Diagram: Implied Volatility

In Figure 2.5, the dashed line (the option value at a point prior to expiration) has greater value than the solid line representing the at-expiration value. Why? Because there is more time for volatility to occur and potentially render intrinsic value. In fact, the more volatility that is expected, the greater the disparity between the two lines at any given moment in time. The option would have greater value if it were thought that higher volatility would be likely in the life of the call. Conversely, if volatility is expected to ebb, the option will be cheaper, and, therefore, the dotted line, representing the call value prior to expiration, will be lower, closer to the at-expiration representation.

P&L Diagram: Time
As time passes, the magnitude of likely price deviations statistically becomes smaller. In other words, an x percent move is less likely to occur if there is one day until expiration than it is if there is, say, one year until expiration. This explains why options lose value as time passes, experiencing time decay. Therefore, as each day passes, the dashed line would move incrementally lower. Eventually, at expiration, the dashed line, representing the option with volatility value, would converge with the at-expiration line. At expiration, there is no more volatility possible in the life of the option and, therefore, no volatility value.

P&L Diagram: Moneyness
The greatest disparity between the values of the option when it has volatility value and at its expiration date is at the price point at which the underlying asset is at the strike price (i.e., when the option is at-the-money). Only when the call is significantly in-the-money or out-of-the-money would the lines converge. Ultimately, at-the-money options have the greatest amount of volatility value because there is the greatest amount of uncertainty as to whether the option will expire in-the-money or out-of-the-money.

The Greeks
Studying incremental risk with a P&L diagram would require measuring shifts in the curve as implied volatility and time change. Interest and dividend changes would also alter the graph. This two-dimensional image is not conducive to a comprehensive analysis. Instead, to study incremental risk, traders use a family of metrics

referred to collectively as "the greeks." Each greek measures incremental changes in one of the option-centric risks. The most commonly used option greeks are delta, gamma, theta, vega, and rho.

Delta

Delta is the rate of change in an option's value relative to a change in the underlying asset.

Delta measures profit or loss as the underlying rises or falls. It is stated as a percent written in decimal form. For example, if an option has a delta of 0.40, it moves 40 percent like the underlying asset (or 40 cents for every $1 move in the underlying asset). Calls, which move in tandem with the underlying asset, have positive deltas. Puts, which are negatively correlated with the underlying asset, have negative deltas. That is to say, when the stock rises, puts lose value; when the stock falls, they gain value.

Delta can be thought of as how much the option acts like the underlying asset. Specific to equity options, it can be thought of as the option position's functionality of an equivalent number of shares of the underlying asset. For example, imagine a 60-delta call. If the call price reacts 60 percent as much as the underlying stock and each option represents 100 shares, the call holder will have a position that profits or loses like 60 shares of that stock. A very deep-in-the-money option will have a delta that approaches 100 and, therefore, functions nearly 100 percent like the underlying asset. A very far out-of-the-money call will have a near zero delta: its price will not change at all as the underlying asset's price moves.

As a rule of thumb, options that are in-the-money have deltas greater than 0.50. The more in-the-money an option, the greater the delta (up to 1.00). Out-of-the-money options generally have deltas less than 0.50. The further out-of-the-money an option, the lower the delta (down to zero). At-the-money options have deltas around 0.50.*

---

*Technically, options that are exactly at-the-money will likely have deltas greater than 0.50, contingent upon time, volatility, interest, and other factors.

Gamma

Gamma is the rate of change of an option's delta given a change in the price of the underlying asset.

When the underlying asset changes in price, relative to the fixed strike price, moneyness—by definition—changes. Therefore, deltas change when the underlying asset rises or falls in price. Sometimes this change can be very significant, especially with large positions. This change is measured by gamma.

Gamma is stated in terms of deltas. Long options have positive gammas; short options have negative gammas. For example, if an option has a gamma of +0.07, if the stock rises $1, the position will gain 7 deltas. If the stock falls, the position will become 7 deltas smaller.

Theta

Theta is the rate of change of an option's value relative to a change in the time remaining to expiration.

Theta measures the rate of time decay. It is stated in dollars and cents per share. For example, if an option has a theta of 0.04, it will lose 4 cents as one day passes (all other factors held constant), which is $4 of actual cash per contract.

An option's theta can change based on many factors, most notably moneyness and time. Short-term at-the-moneys have the highest thetas. Thetas get bigger for at-the-money options as time passes. This is sometimes referred to as the "nonlinear rate of time decay." In-the-money and out-of-the-money options, which have smaller thetas, have more constant thetas as time passes.

Vega

Vega is the rate of change of an option's value relative to a change in implied volatility.

Vega is stated in dollars and cents, just like theta. When implied volatility rises or falls, the option value changes by the amount of the vega. Long options have positive vegas (i.e., positive correlation to volatility changes); short options have negative vegas, therefore, they have a negative correlation to volatility changes.

For example, if an option has a vega of +0.10, for each 1 point implied volatility rises, the option gains 10 cents in value. For each 1 point implied volatility falls, the option loses 10 cents of value.

Long-term options have higher vegas than short-term options. And at-the-money options have bigger vegas than both in-the-money or out-of-the-money options. Vegas for all options tend to get smaller as time passes.

Rho

Rho is the rate of change of an option's value relative to a change in interest rates.

Rho is stated in dollars and cents. For example, an option that has a rho of +0.20 will gain 20 cents if interest rates were to rise 1 full percentage point.* If interest rates were to fall 1 full percent, the option would lose 20 cents.

Calls have positive rhos; puts have negative rhos. Because the effect of interest loses relevance with decreased time, rho moves toward zero as time passes.

The Greeks: Independent Influences

Each greek is isolated and moves independently from the others. For example, a given option position may profit from delta, lose from theta, and profit from vega. Because each of these valuation metrics has its own command over option values, each metric must be monitored.

---

*It is more common to see interest rates change by a quarter percent, or 25 basis points at a time.

3

C H A P T E R

SPREADING RISK

Many people are unaware of this fact: *maintaining a floor-trader position requires constant monitoring.* Market making is a highly engaging trading style. There is no rest for the wicked in this game. An instant can make or break a floor trader's week, month, or sometimes year: go to lunch and you can miss the opportunity of a lifetime; or a surprise adverse move can happen that can cost tens of thousands of dollars. Monitoring a market-maker position is like watching a toddler who has just learned to walk and who has an affinity for sticking things into electrical outlets.

There are many wild stories on the trading floor—most of which likely are true. Throughout my career on the floor, I heard this recurring story about how, on busy days, some traders would affix a plastic bag to themselves into which they would urinate to avoid having to leave the trading floor to go to the bathroom.

Knowing the floor-trader mindset and what the trade-offs are for not being there when the important trades go down, I imagine there is some truth to this floor lore. Personally, I've never tried it, but I have to admit, the thought had crossed my mind. *I just couldn't figure out how to attach the bag.*

If a trader plans to be away from trading for more than a day, conventional wisdom is for the trader to "get flat"—to eliminate all the position risk. This is easier said than done. Market makers absorb liquidity and can't always close open contracts without taking a loss. Active market makers could have tens of thousands of options in their inventory. Having to take a loss on that many contracts—even just a penny per contract—could make for an expensive vacation before even leaving town.

So what do traders do to minimize risk? They spread. Spreading has many functions, but the primary function of spreading is to minimize risk.

SPREADING

A spread is a position that consists of two or more different components, called "legs." In its simplest form, a spread is a position consisting of two different options. Some spreads can be very complex, consisting of hundreds of different series. Spreads may also include the underlying asset (a stock position and an option on that stock, for example). There are seemingly endless ways that option spreads can be created. But, again, the primary motivation of a spread is to reduce risk. That is done by shaping position risk into something altogether new that is, in one way or another, more advantageous than the sum of its parts.

Spreads can be either intraclass or interclass. An *intraclass spread* is a spread consisting of legs that are listed on the same underlying asset. For example, a trader may buy a Netflix, Inc. (NFLX) November 165 call and, at the same time, sell a NFLX November 170 call. Intraclass spreads are the most common exchange-traded spreads, especially among retail traders.

An *interclass spread* is a spread consisting of components listed on two or more different underlying assets. A common example is the notes over bonds spread (NOB), traded in the financial futures options. NOB traders will buy or sell options in the U.S. Treasury notes options and, at the same time, take an offsetting position in U.S. Treasury bond options. Interclass spreading is more common among professional traders and institutions.

Why Spread?

Having a mastery of spreads is essential for both market makers and market takers. Spreads give traders a choice of both how to trade (in terms of flexibility) and what to trade (in terms of asset class). The market exposure of a spread is different from that of its individual components. Furthermore, each spread is unique in its risk structure. Positions that have similar but not identical exposure can be created by crafting spreads consisting of different components. For example, a bullish trader can buy a call, buy a call spread, sell a put, sell a put spread, trade a ratio spread (calls or puts), sell a covered call, buy a directional butterfly, buy a directional time spread, or pursue a host of other strategies.

There are a large number of spread choices for traders who have a given forecast on an underlying asset. Traders have a choice among different spread strategies, as well as many choices as to which month(s) to trade and which strike(s) to trade within each spread type.

Spread Selection and Edge

For any given market condition, the structure of one spread has a superior risk-reward to that of others. Clever traders use strategy selection to their advantage by selecting the alternative that provides the lowest risk of loss and highest profit potential, while factoring in the odds of success.

For example, if a trader expects the underlying asset to rise to a specific price point over the next few weeks, the trader would rather buy a one-month call spread with the short (sold) strike coinciding with resistance. Set up like this, the spread would offer an advantage over other strategies such as an outright call. If a trader is only tepidly bullish and believes that implied volatility is high, she'd likely opt to sell a short-term, out-of-the-money put spread, giving up some potential delta appreciation, as a result of negative gamma, in favor of gaining short implied volatility exposure while maximizing the chance of success. If a speculative trader thinks a stock will rise sharply in a short time period, simply buying a short-term, out-of-the-money call can be the best play of choice.

This is one way in which non-market-maker traders can gain an edge. All option trades have some degree of exposure to direction, time, underlying volatility, implied volatility, and perhaps interest. Skillful traders strive to exploit all these option-pricing factors on each and every trade. Traders should select from at least three different spread trade setups to select the one that best matches his or her outlook in terms of each of the relevant pricing factors. Skillful traders who consider all the pricing exposures of an option position gain an advantage—that is, an edge—over those who don't.

OPTION-CENTRIC RISK AND ASSET CLASS

By extension, option spreads also make it possible for traders to trade an asset class that they otherwise wouldn't be capable of trading: volatility. Notwithstanding the discussion in the previous section, each option trade can ultimately be distilled down to two exposures: direction and volatility. Again, direction risk is measured in terms of delta. Volatility exposure, then, can be broken down into two categories, realized volatility risk (measured by the risk pair of gamma and theta) and implied volatility (measured by vega).

Linear trading vehicles, such as stocks, ETFs, or futures, don't have a volatility component to their value. The exposure of linear vehicles is measured entirely by delta. Specifically, their delta is 1.00 per unit (100 shares for stocks, generally one contract for futures, etc.). They have no gamma, theta, or vega. Gamma, theta, and vega are purely option-centric risks.

Option traders always have volatility exposure—whether it is their intent or not. That is to say, each option position will have a realized volatility bias and an implied volatility bias. Positions that have bullish realized volatility have positive (long) gamma and negative theta. Those that have bearish realized volatility have negative (short) gamma and positive theta. Likewise, trades that have bullish implied volatility have positive (long) vega. And those that have bearish implied volatility have negative (short) vega.

Traders can actively take positions in both realized and implied volatility. This makes volatility, in and of itself, a veritable asset class. While all traders may be able to benefit from volatility, option traders—and only option traders—can actually trade volatility.

SPREADS AND MARKET-MAKER ARBITRAGE

Spreading also provides a framework for market makers to price options. All options listed on the same underlying asset have an inherent correlation. This correlation is the result of the substitutability of similar contracts and is discussed in greater detail in Chapter 13.

In some ways, the interrelationship of option values makes option trading easier than trading linear assets. Although options are arguably more complex in nature than, say, a stock or a future, the valuation of spreads provides a framework for trading. When the value of one option is known, it can be used as a "lean" to price other options. Traders can trade spreads at favorable prices by "leaning on" one leg of the spread, opportunistically lying in wait for the other leg's price to change and cause the spread price to get out of line. When they do, the trader can execute the spread in its entirety for either an arbitrage profit or at least for a favorable trade price.

SPREAD CATEGORIES

There are four general categories into which all spreads fall: vertical spreads, time spreads, straddles and strangles, and synthetics.

Vertical Spreads
A *vertical spread* is a spread consisting of either two calls or two puts, both on the same underlying asset, sharing the same expiration month, but with a different strike price. For example:

Buy one XYZ January 110–120 call spread at 6.00.

In this spread, a trader would buy one XYZ January 110 call and at the same time sell one XYZ January 120 call and pay a total debit of 6. The credit collected for selling the 120 call helps offset the premium paid for the 110 call.

In the professional-trading nomenclature, vertical spreads are divided into two categories: call spreads or put spreads. There are, then, four possible mutations that traders can trade:

- Buy a call spread.
- Sell a call spread.
- Buy a put spread.
- Sell a put spread.

Nonprofessional traders use a different vernacular for vertical spread categorization, contrary to the simple buying or selling of call spreads or put spreads. Retail traders commonly divide vertical spreads into either debit and credit spreads or bull and bear spreads.

Debit and credit spreads are sorted as such because of the posting to a trader's account when the trade is made. When the more expensive option is purchased, in either a call or put spread, and the cheaper option is sold, a debit results (i.e., the trader pays for the spread, hoping it can be sold later at a higher price) in the trader's account. Hence the name *debit spread*.

When the higher-priced option is sold, in either a call of put spread, and the less expensive one is purchased, a credit results (i.e., the trader receives cash in his or her account, hoping to later pay less than the credit received to close the trade). Hence the name *credit spread*.

Alternatively, directional exposure can be used as a segregator in the retail realm. Call or put spreads that profit from the underlying asset rising are called "bull call spreads" or "bull put spreads," respectively. Call or put spreads that profit from the underlying asset falling in price are called "bear call spreads" or "bear put spreads," respectively.

Vertical spreads are one of the most powerful and versatile categories of option spreads. They can be used to trade directional exposure, time exploitation, volatility revaluation, and more. They can be very conservative or very leveraged plays. While elegant in their simple construction, they are fairly intricate spreads that require a thorough understanding to trade effectively.

Ratio vertical spreads, which include backspreads, are an extension of vertical spreads. As opposed to the accustomed one-to-one proportion of the component options of vertical spreads, ratio vertical spreads, as the name implies, have a ratio of options bought to options sold other than one-to-one. These are sometimes called one-by-twos, one-by-threes, or whatever the option ratio dictates. For example, a trader may trade the XYZ November 20–22.50 call spread one-by-two, by buying one November 20 call and selling two November 22.50 calls.

Ratio spreads can be created in any proportion. Generally, a greater number of the lower-priced options are traded in order to create a lower-risk trade. It is commonplace to refer to trading ratio spreads that result in debits as "buying the spread," and those that result in a credit as "selling the spread."

Time Spreads

A *time spread* is a spread consisting of either two calls or two puts, both on the same underlying asset, sharing the same strike price, but with a different expiration month. For example:

Buy one XYZ March–April 50 call spread at 2.30.

In this spread, the trader would buy one April 50 call and sell one March 50 call for a net debit of 2.30.

Time spreads are also called "calendar spreads" or, archaically, "horizontal spreads." In giving an order to trade a time spread, it is customary for traders to say they are buying the spread if they are buying the month with more time until expiration—which would be the more expensive option resulting in a debit for the transaction. Traders say they are selling the spread if they are selling the longer-dated option, again being more expensive and therefore resulting, in this case, in a credit.

A trader placing an order in a professional-trading environment would simply say something like, "Buy one May–June 70 put." In a nonprofessional trading environment, one would say, "Buy one May–June 70 put time [or calendar] spread."

Time spreads are useful strategies that are traded by both professional and retail traders. Professional traders tend to trade time spreads as a volatility differential trade, buying the low volatility month and selling the high. Retail people are more fixated on always buying the spread, sometimes disregarding the volatility levels, with the objective of benefiting from the time-decay disparity of options with different expiration dates.

Other common option spreads that fit into the time-spread family are double calendars, diagonals, and double diagonals:

- *Double calendars* consist of two time spreads entered at the same time, creating a four-legged option strategy—long (or short) the two longer-dated options and short (or long) the two shorter-dated options. Double calendars consist of two common strike prices. Double calendars are sometimes also called "strangle swaps" when one spread (the lower-strike spread) is a put calendar and the other (the higher-strike spread) is a call calendar.

- *Diagonals* are made up of two options that both have different expiration months and different strikes. Diagonals are called such as they are a combination of a vertical and a horizontal spread. In retail trading it is most common to buy the lower-strike, longer-dated call option and sell a higher-strike, shorter-dated call. The construction of diagonal spreads is more assorted in professional-trading circuits.

- *Double diagonals* consist of two diagonal spreads held at the same time. It is most common—especially in retail trading—for there to be two months involved in the spread and four separate strike prices. This spread may involve a combination of calls and puts.

Straddles and Strangles

A *straddle* consists of a long put and a long call (or a short put and a short call) sharing the same strike and the same expiration month. Similarly, a *strangle* consists of a long put and a long call (or a short put and a short call) each with different strikes. Typically the put in a strangle has a lower strike (and is usually out-of-the-money at the onset of the trade) than the call (which is usually also out-of-the-money when the trade is established).

Once again, the assumption is that spreads reduce risk. One could argue that neither straddles nor strangles reduce risk. In terms of incremental risk, theta, gamma, and vega all increase to around double that of either individual leg of the spread. Delta generally gets offset, but the volatility risk is doubled. For that reason, there are some traders, albeit a minority, who don't consider straddles or strangles to be spreads.

Straddles and strangles are volatility plays. The straddle, in particular, is the purest way to buy or sell volatility. This is evidenced in the fact that both gamma and vega are maximized by buying or selling both spread legs and that profits or losses can increase with great magnitude if there is a volatile move in either direction.

Synthetics

Put-call parity is a formula that expresses the relationship of calls to puts. But much more can be derived from this concise equation. It also suggests option relationships, called "synthetics." The following is the formula for put-call parity*:

$$Call = Put + Stock - Strike + Interest - Dividend$$

To rephrase in a nonmathematical vernacular, this equation states that once interest and dividends are factored in, a call equals a put of the same strike plus stock. Mathematically,

$$Call = Put + Stock$$

Specifically,

$$Long\ Call = Long\ Put + Long\ Stock$$

A long put combined with long stock is a basic spread. Changing the signs in the equation yields important algebraic restatements of this relationship with which to create other spreads. Some synthetic spreads contain stock, some only options. Synthetics help traders in arbitrage trading as well as in understanding positions in simpler terms. Synthetics are discussed in greater detail in Chapter 11.

---

*Specifically, put-call parity is for European exercise–style options.

SPREADS, SPREAD NAMES, AND TRADING PHILOSOPHY

The four spread categories are the general classifications of option spreads; however, there are a seemingly infinite number of unique individual spreads that can be traded. All spreads fall into one or more of these four classifications. Some people seemingly spend a lifetime trying to achieve the goal of learning all the different individual spreads, one spread at a time. With the great magnitude of unique spreads that can be created with options, as one can see, this may not be the best means of spread mastery.

The problem is that many times aspiring spreaders, especially in the nonprofessional sphere, focus on the wrong things. They get caught up in the individuality of each spread: the segregation of spreads by name, their at-expiration diagrams, the "rules" for each spread. *They focus on the limitations of each individual spread.* Having been reared as a trader on the exchange floor, I, like many of my peers, have had a different approach to learning spreads. Floor people tend to focus on spreading as a single technique that is part of a holistic approach to trading, *not* on a fragmented series of different strategies.

After many years of trading professionally, I started working often with retail traders as a lecturer. When I first started on the lecture circuit, the market was somewhat stable, and the trade du jour was the iron condor (a four-legged strategy that profits in low-volatility environments). Therefore, I found myself giving presentation after presentation on the iron condor strategy.

Around that time, I was talking with a professional trader I knew who worked for a proprietary trading firm that traded volatility arbitrage—high-level stuff. Incidentally, this firm was a major, extremely successful option player in the United States (in other words, a company filled with *really good traders*). This trader from that firm asked what I had been up to lately. I told him about how I was off to some city to give a presentation on iron condors. His reply: "What's an iron condor?"

It wasn't that this trader was unknowledgeable in options. On the contrary, he was one of the most successful, and smartest, traders I knew. It's that the iron condor isn't as revered in the professional trading circles as it is with retail traders. This trader focused mainly on straddles, synthetics, and creative approaches to risk management. He likely traded iron condors in his career, probably many times without knowing the name of the strategy. If so, he probably just piecemealed it together because it happened to have the right risk profile for his situation. Good option traders fit the trade to the outlook; amateurs fit the outlook to the trade. And that is the difference.

Professional traders and clever stay-at-home traders find the absolute risk and incremental risk desired for a particular scenario and create an option position that fits their forecast. They focus on exposures in direction, time, volatility, and perhaps interest rates—that is, the exposures measured by the option greeks—and construct a position to exploit them.

SPREAD PHILOSOPHY AND METHODOLOGY

An ordered methodology of trade selection is also important in the philosophy of spreading. One of the biggest problems I see with new traders is that they learn only a small handful of spreads and cling to them. They are then forced to find underlying instruments that match what they know how to do. This limits traders two ways. It is limiting in the number of available vehicles to trade; but more important, it is limiting in how the trader can subsequently manage the position once it is established.

It is common for traders to adjust positions. Adjusting means changing a spread to alter its risk profile. This may include rolling (closing one leg of a spread and opening a new leg to create a new spread altogether), augmenting, shrinking, or changing the spread in some other way. Traders must always carry a position that matches the trader's outlook. When their outlook changes, the position must either be closed or adjusted.

If the trader only knows a handful of strategies, he or she could be unfamiliar with any newly created strategies resulting from adjusting. The trader will be ill prepared to deal with risk. Therefore, the objective is not to try and master many different types of spreads. Traders need to master *options*. The rest falls into place.

C H A P T E R

AN OPTION BY ANY OTHER NAME

As a market maker, you can't help but feel as if you are always look-ing over your shoulder. In the process of buying bids and selling offers, market makers accumulate positions, any of which may come to bite them in their proverbial behind in any multitude of ways. For example, market makers might be short gamma in one option class that can lead to a disaster if a large, unexpected move occurs. They may have too much negative theta in another option class and be unable to reduce the position before the three days of weekend time decay comes out. Or market makers might have too much long or short vega in an option class, which can be detrimen-tal if implied volatility moves the wrong way in either case.

To survive and prosper, all option traders live and die by the greeks. For non-liquidity providers, the greeks provide the clearest way to see a holistic view of position risk. For market makers, it is the only way possible to manage large, accumulated, multistrike positions.

Early in my career when I was a clerk in the CBOT's Bond Room, I clerked for a rather demanding, intense trader. A main function of my job was to pick up his "cards"—which were cards on which traders would write their trades to be passed along to the clearing firm to notify them of the transaction details. Before turning in the cards to keypunch, I would first type the trade information into the computer system and generate a *position run* that showed long and short options at each strike; option and underlying prices; monetary risk should a standard deviation movement in the underlying asset occur; P&L; and, of course, the position greeks. Most important, I was to verify the information on the position run; I had to be right.

One day was the busiest I'd ever seen in the bond option pit. The trader for whom I worked was shoving handfuls of cards at me every few minutes. I ran back and forth, punching in cards at the computer at the desk, verifying the data to see that it was accurate and made sense, ran it to the trader, and got more cards: *wash, rinse, repeat.*

In the midst of the action on this day, an unfortunate thing happened: the computer went down. And, when I say "an unfortunate thing," I mean a *really* unfortunate thing. The date was around 1995, and this occurrence required calling someone from the computer department to come and figure out what went wrong. It would be a half hour or more until we were up and running again. *This was a problem.*

In trading, the show must go on. The trader for whom I worked had a position—a large position—and needed to know his risk to know where problems could arise, how to spread out of current risk, and how to adjust his bids and offers to balance his position; basically, he needed the information in the computer to avoid potential disaster, and I couldn't access it.

Preparing for the worst, I took a deep breath, walked into the pit, and calmly explained that the computer was down and I wasn't sure how long it would take to get fixed and that I didn't know what his position was.

I learned a couple of things that day. For one, I learned that even when you think you're preparing for the worst, the situation can work out much worse than you ever thought possible. But rivaling this lesson for most important one of the day, I learned that the data spit out from the computer wasn't quite as mysterious and esoteric as I'd thought up until that point.

The trader explained to me (rather loudly, with much profanity) that I was to bring him his position greeks, even if I needed to calculate it by hand, *which I did*.

Each option has an associated delta, gamma, theta, vega, and rho. The greeks of a spread, even of a large complex spread (i.e., position) like that of a market maker, is merely an aggregate of each greek of all the individual options that are components of the spread. It was, therefore, a fairly simple process—tedious, but simple—to take the delta, gamma, theta, and vega of each individual option of each trade, multiply each by the number of contracts in the trade, and add this sum to the existing position, adjusted to the new underlying price.

OPTION-PRICING MODELS

The greeks are a by-product of an option-pricing model. Option-pricing models take a series of inputs and generate an option's theoretical value. Some of these inputs are also used to calculate the greeks. The model inputs needed for different asset classes are about the same, with perhaps one difference: dividends. All conventional listed American or European options have these five model inputs: strike price, underlying asset price, time to expiration, interest, and volatility. Equity options may also include a dividend variable as a sixth input.

VARIOUS MODELS

Option-pricing models used to be a somewhat esoteric tool practical only for professional traders and academics. Nowadays, option-pricing models are ubiquitous and readily usable by all. At the time of this writing, a Google search for the phrase *option-pricing model* returned 1.3 million results.

The contemporary nonprofessional's ability to efficiently use option-pricing models is a result of two main variables: (1) the development of modern technology and information transfer to more efficiently integrate the model into a retail trader's trading routine, and (2) the fact that an increased number of models and trading platforms integrating models have been created, some specifically for the general public.

The first widely accepted option-pricing model was introduced in 1973, and it is referred to as the Black-Scholes model. The Black-Scholes model calculates theoretical values for options on European-exercise, non-dividend-paying stocks. Based on the efforts of Fisher Black and Myron Scholes, the model's creators, more option-pricing models explaining the price behavior of options soon cropped up. Nowadays, there are many different models available for traders' use. All serve the same purpose—generating theoretical values and, by association, greeks. But each has a different approach and therefore yields slightly different results.

In the retail-trading realm, the Black-Scholes model is still often used to value European-exercise options, such as many U.S. index options contracts. For U.S. equity options, which are American-exercise style, retail traders often use the binomial pricing model. This model, and a few others, is widely available for use free of charge online in simple, easy-to-use interfaces.

Professional traders, especially those who are part of a group that can capitalize on economies of scale, tend to use more advanced models—sometimes even proprietary trading models developed in-house. In many cases, the difference is what is overlaid on the models to fine-tune the relative prices of all options listed on the same underlying. One of the major considerations is volatility skew.

VOLATILITY SKEW

The implied volatility of different options listed on the same underlying asset needn't be the same. In fact, it seldom is. This phenomenon is called "volatility skew." Volatility skew can be thought of two different ways: (1) how volatility differs among the listed expiration months, and (2) how volatility differs among the available strike prices.

Term Structure of Volatility

The volatility disparity among the available expiration months is called the "term structure of volatility," horizontal skew, or monthly skew. If one considers that implied volatility is the market's demand for and supply of options—holding all other option pricing factors constant—it follows that there may be different implied volatilities for each expiration cycle. For example, if over the next few days an important announcement were expected to hit the news wire for a particular stock, traders would likely buy the short-term options (therefore, driving up their price) and ignore the more expensive longer-term options that encompass more time than is needed in the life of the trade.

Conversely, if a major announcement is expected in, say, three months, traders may buy the three- or four-month options that coincide with the expected time horizon of the volatility event, driving up the implied volatility in that expiration month. The shorter-term options' (those with less than three months until expiration) implied volatility would likely remain steady or even decline if the market thinks the stock will remain stable until the news is released.

Term structure can vary greatly. Sometimes volatility disparities can be profound, with 10, 20, or more points of volatility difference. Sometimes they can be more subtle, being only a point difference or less. Generally the difference has to do with the timing of expectations for volatility events, but sometimes other factors come into play.

Vertical Skew

Vertical skew is the difference in implied volatility among the various strikes listed within a single expiration month. Vertical skew is sometimes called "strike skew." Like horizontal skew, vertical skew is also a function of the supply and demand for options that serve slightly different purposes. Though all the options of the same type listed within the same expiration cycle are somewhat substitutable for one another, the subtle differences inherent in their moneyness make them more or less desirable given certain market psychology and criteria.

One of the main influences for vertical skew is fear. With equity options (as well as with many ETF options and stock index options) the fear is to the downside. The market, collectively, is long stocks. After a company issues stock, the shares are held by an individual or institution—*someone owns it*. Though some traders may short the stock, they sell it to someone else who then owns it. Shares of stock exist. Options, particularly puts, can protect these shares against losses resulting from the stock price falling. Therefore, out-of-the-money puts (or, by the synthetic relationship, in-the-money calls) tend to have higher implied volatility than other options in the same expiration month on the same stock.

Conversely, out-of-the-money calls (and, synthetically related, in-the-money puts) tend to have lower implied volatility. This results from the innate complacency associated with stable or rising markets. In these market scenarios, investors tend to sell out-of-the-money covered calls (a spread consisting of long stock and a short call) because if the stock falls, the calls are not a detriment. (In fact, they provide some cushion, counteracting some of the loss on the stock price.) If the stock is stable, the covered call trader earns a profit on the call as it expires. And if the stock rises, the trader also earns a profit (though he or she may give up some upside appreciation). This short-call bias puts downward pressure on options with strikes higher than the stock price; hence, skew.

Other assets may have a vertical skew that is different from the skew in equity options. For example, agricultural options tend to have fear to the upside. If grain prices rise, grain elevators and food processors must pay more. Rising grain prices is an inflationary factor. Therefore, some grain options hedgers tend to bid up the upside options.

VOLATILITY, SKEW, AND PRICING MODELS

In practical use, option-pricing models require the trader to input an implied volatility figure that "fits" the market. The theoretical value is calculated so that it sits between the bid and offer to reflect current market value; hence, the name *implied volatility*—it is the volatility implied by the market.

The assumed output of the model, option value, is generally known; it is the volatility input that needs to be determined. The option value should, logically, lie between the bid and the offer. The market (collectively) wants to buy at the bid; therefore, value must be above the bid—the market wants to pay less than the option is worth. Likewise, the market wants to sell at the offer; therefore, the option must be worth less.

Traders—especially active professional traders—need to know the volatility values of every option listed on the option class they trade. The volatilities among the strike prices tend to have a specific relationship. The volatilities either linearly or exponentially rise or fall with each successive strike in a sloping fashion. Vertical skew, then, is explained by *up slopes* and *down slopes*.

Many of the more advanced models automatically calculate the vertical volatility skew for each successive strike by means of the trader inputting a single volatility variable and adding an up-slope variable and a down-slope variable. The single volatility input is typically the implied volatility of the at-the-money strike (though this is not always the case). The up slope then calculates successively higher or lower volatility inputs for the calculation of the theoretical value for options with strike prices higher than the at-the-money. The down slope calculates incrementally higher or lower volatility inputs used to calculate the theoretical values of options struck lower than at-the-money.

Again, these calculations generate volatilities for each strike either linearly or exponentially. Traders "line up" the slopes to fit the market, ensuring that theoretical values accurately reflect market values. This is particularly important for active traders with big positions.

SKEW, SLOPES, AND THE GREEKS

Recall that the values of each option greek are contingent upon inputs used in the pricing model. And, of course, the theoretical value generated is likewise a direct product of the mathematics of the model. Market makers, and other arbitrageurs, must take special care to ensure that the slope values are correct. If the slope inputs are incorrect, two problems arise: (1) the theoretical values generated will be incorrect, leading to mispriced individual options and mispriced spreads, and (2) the greeks will be incorrect, inhibiting proper position management.

Let's Talk Tails

Depending on the particular model used and the mathematics of the slope calculations, variant results in values and greeks will be returned. Comparing different models' calculations on the same option class can show disagreements in the theoretical values and greeks throughout the chain. Evidence of the discrepancies of alternative models is observable, particularly in how the "tails" of the probability curve are calculated.

Many models assume a lognormal distribution of stock prices. However, it is generally accepted by many in the trading community that a standard lognormal distribution is not representative of reality. Highly unlikely statistical events (e.g., three, four, and five standard deviation price moves) have historically occurred in the stock market much more frequently than a standard lognormal curve would indicate.

The empirical observation indicates a *leptokurtic* distribution. That means the tails of the probability distribution curve are fatter—that is, they have a greater probability of multistandard deviation moves—than a customary lognormal curve used by a typical pricing model. Advanced models compensate for the shortcomings of the unadulterated models by adjusting the volatilities of the slopes to fit the observed leptokurtosis of actual price movements.

Importance of Having the Right Volatility Inputs

If the volatility inputs are wrong (either for the at-the-moneys or the far out-of-the-moneys residing at the tails of the curve), both theoretical values and the greeks will be wrong. The precision of theoretical values is very important—particularly to professional traders. Market makers and other arbitrageurs buy below and sell above theoreticals to generate theoretical edge. If the values are incorrect, the trader may unknowingly trade for negative theoretical edge—an obvious problem. But let's examine more closely the implications of generating incorrect greeks.

Imagine a scenario in which an equity option trader uses a volatility assumption that is slightly misrepresentative of actual market values. When volatility rises, it makes the deltas of all options move toward 0.50. That means out-of-the-money options' deltas increase and in-the-money options' deltas decrease. Conversely, when volatility falls, deltas move away from 0.50. So out-of-the-money options' deltas move lower toward zero and in-the-money options rise toward 1.00. So a wrong volatility can have drastic consequences on position deltas, particularly for large positions.

Example
Say the trader was short the following position:

> With Apple Inc. (AAPL) at $289 . . .
> Short 500 Jan. 310 calls at 11.90 (Volatility = 32, call delta = –0.38)

Each call has a delta of –0.38. The delta on the 500-lot position, then, is –190, which is equivalent to the directional sensitivity of being short 19,000 shares (500 times 0.38 times 100).

If the trader erroneously used a lower volatility of, say, 29, for the 310 strike (perhaps as a result of an incorrect slope), the delta would be lower, calculated at –0.36 per contract. On the 500-lot, that's a total delta of –180, or the sensitivity of being short 18,000 shares.

A difference of 1,000 deltas' worth of price sensitivity can drastically misguide the trader's expectations and, by extension, his or her position management. A $10 move in AAPL stock would mean making or losing $10,000 that isn't indicated by the delta because of the discrepancy of short 19,000 versus short 18,000 deltas. Further, if this position is hedged, the hedge will be incorrect by 1,000 deltas. The trader may think he's flat but would, in fact, be mishedged—potentially leading to unexpected gains or losses.

Gamma, theta, and vega can all be off as well as delta with an improper volatility or slope input. The differences in the greeks resulting from alternate volatility inputs are a function of multiple criteria. For example, an at-the-money option will have lower theta and higher gamma given a lower volatility input. But the effect is less on in-the-money or out-of-the-money options. The effect of volatility on the greeks is very important to understand, but it is not always intuitive.

HANGING AROUND AFTER HOURS

I began my trading career as well prepared as anyone could be. I can attribute much of my readiness to how I spent my free time during my clerking years. At that point in my life, I had no wife, no kids, only a (lousy) part-time job to supplement my rather inadequate clerk salary so I could pay the rent.

For a good stretch of time, I would spend an hour or two after the market close each day up in the office of the firm for which I worked tinkering with the pricing model user interface. It was a proprietary system created by the firm. Again, these were not widely available in the early 1990s. Now, any options-friendly retail brokerage firm offers such an interface (and, typically a better interface than the one I used back then) as part of its trading platform at no cost to its customers.

At the computer, I'd create practice trades and manage them as if they were real. I would enter trades at market prices. And I'd wargame situations: I'd change the date to move time forward and see how the P&L and greeks reacted. I'd change volatility. I'd move the price of the underlying. And I'd change the slopes. All the while I'd quiz myself, trying to guess correctly how the position would react to the given changes.

This private practice lab was a part of my learning process for a long time. I was very disciplined about mastering the model. I found it fascinating. And, it proved to be some of the best training I could have gotten. While theory and academia are essential, there was nothing like the hands-on learning of watching prices in action in my trading microcosm.

CAVEATS AND INSPIRATION

Learning the functionality of the model is essential. But one must consider it for what it is: *a model*. It is applied mathematics designed to explain reality. This observation should serve as both a caveat and an inspiration.

After spending much time preparing to be a trader and learning just about everything I could as a clerk, I found myself taking my first step into the pit as a member of the exchange. I started trading as a market maker on the floor of the CBOE in 1998. I quickly began amassing positions—large positions—and subsequently managing them. Though, as a clerk, I had stress tested the model in every way possible, I found that sometimes, in reality, option positions acted slightly differently than one would expect, relying only on the model. There was a learning curve once becoming a trader as well.

I started out making markets in one equity option class—those of the Ford Motor Company (F). Then I soon added another stock to my repertoire. Then another. Soon enough I had 10, then 20 option classes to trade. Though the individual underlying equities were from different industries and had different business models and different price action, adding a new option class was fairly seamless.

Trading options on one asset is like trading options on any other asset. The pricing model doesn't know the name of the stock, the industry, or what its chart looks like: it only knows the numbers. Being a successful option trader is a matter of understanding how options work, with all their nuances and quirks. The underlying asset is to some degree irrelevant.

In fact, it was common for market makers to migrate from pits that got slow and lost volume to more lively pits when market conditions changed. Most of my career was spent in the Ford pit making markets in the option classes traded there. It was an active pit for a number of years. However, when market conditions changed, I moved around a bit. At one point, when the equity-option trading business slowed significantly, I moved to the Chicago Board of Trade and traded corn options. It would seem that corn and car makers are two very different things—and they are. Trading their options, however, is pretty much about the same.

5

THE ZEN OF TRADING AND HOPING TO NEVER GET A REAL JOB

At one point in my life, I knew almost no one who had what I would call a "real job." As a professional trader, ingrained in the trading culture, I spent a fair amount of the time of my adult life with other traders, both professionally and socially. I must admit (and I'm self-aware enough to realize) that traders are an interesting breed. The business of trading is equally fascinating—different from any other. Many of us who have borne the moniker of professional trader would agree that trading is not a "real job."

Professional traders are not like the typical corporate employees toiling in cubicles, living by political correctness, laughing at their superiors' (unfunny) jokes in the hopes of getting ahead—*playing the game*. Traders have one goal and one goal only: *make a profit*. If they achieve that goal, they are successful.

Some traders are sole proprietors who don't have bosses. And for those who work for a firm, their bosses tend to leave them alone as long as they are making money. As a floor trader, I went through stretches of time lasting weeks, maybe months, without ever seeing my boss—and I liked it that way. Most traders have no one's proverbial butt to kiss. No one cares about the trader's manners, mannerisms, education, background, personal hygiene, or what-have-yous. If the trader can make money, he or she is good trader. It's a bottom-line business. You go down to the floor (or office), try and make money, and then go home. A *real job*? Debatable.

THE PRIDE OF RAND

It is very fortunate for some people in the trading community that they never had to have the dreaded "real job." They may not have survived on the "outside." The members of the trading community all come from very diverse backgrounds. But they are bound together by the common goal of trying to figure out the market and make money from it.

Trading options can be somewhat cerebral; traders have to be smart. But that doesn't mean they're a bunch of Ivy Leaguers. Where a trader went to school, his or her pedigree, or family lineage is irrelevant. The trading industry is capitalism at its finest. If you have the wherewithal to make money as a trader, there is nothing that can stop you. If you don't, there is nothing that can help you.

It is the pure pursuit of profit that drives traders to success (which, incidentally, indirectly provides the service of liquidity for the common good) coupled with unadulterated ability. *Ayn Rand would be proud.* Some have what it takes; some do not. There are plenty of people who came from nothing, who couldn't afford to go to expensive schools, but who were smart enough to make it as successful traders.

When I was a clerk and was trying to decide whether or not I wanted to pursue a career in trading, I asked a trader I knew if he liked his chosen profession. His response: "What else am I going to do?" This was one of the biggest power brokers in the pit—a huge trader. He came from a humble background with no formal education. But he was sharp, highly aggressive, and very boisterous—he had a strong "pit presence." Frankly, he was right. He probably wouldn't fit in elsewhere in society. But he was right at home on the trading floor. *A big fish in the pond of opportunity.*

And there were plenty of people from unexpected backgrounds who carved out careers in the options industry. People I traded with were former car salespeople, professional gamblers, bartenders, politicians, and pig farmers. There were also those from former high-powered, intellectual or otherwise impressive careers such as entrepreneurs, doctors, engineers, and world-record holders. And there were those from miscellaneous walks of life too: real estate people, professional athletes, artists, and—oh, yes—a few finance graduates. Again, the only constant among floor denizens was the lust for mastering the market.

THE BEST (AND WORST) JOB IN THE WORLD

Though being a professional trader hardly has the feel of a real job, it is an occupation in its own right that requires the discipline and diligence of any other profession—maybe more so than other professions. Perhaps it is conceivable that, in some sense of the word, one might call it a job—all semantics aside. That being said, the career path of a trader is truly the best job in the world at times; and alas, sometimes it's the worst job in the world. It's a left-brained game of numbers that can be highly right-brained emotional. In lots of cases, the difference between love or hate for the job can come down to whether the last trade was a winner or a loser.

There are some benefits and detriments to being a career trader. The hours can be great. The grain market, for example, is open from 9:30 a.m. to 1:15 p.m. Central Time—less than a four-hour day. Bond traders need to be up early, starting at 7:20. But they're done by 2:00. Even equity option traders are done by 3:00 in Chicago. When the bell rings, there's not much else to do but go home. Further, traders control their own destiny. No politics, just the task at hand. And the compensation can be substantial. There are many traders under 30 years old who pull in six or possibly even seven figures a year.

But, it can be difficult to remove one's self from the day's activity—it's hard for a trader not to take his or her work home. Lots can go wrong. Some troubles are within the trader's control. Some cannot be controlled. There is empowerment in relying on oneself to survive and prosper, but the bad days—and there are bad days—can be emotionally taxing. Some days I'd come home with gifts of diamonds for my wife; some days we'd talk about selling the furniture to pay the rent.

OTHER PEOPLE'S MONEY

For a lot of people, overcoming the psychological aspect of trading can be a big hurdle to success. The psychology is different for traders who trade for themselves than it is for traders who trade someone else's money. It's easy for traders who trade for themselves to be overly cautious in their trading. After all, some option positions can have unlimited risk. And professional traders, market makers in particular, need to trade big to compete. A lot of money is on the line for the active market maker. Traders need to play it tight. But trading with too much fear can be detrimental to success. It can paralyze some traders, causing them to miss out on exploiting reasonable-risk opportunities. For some traders, working for a trading group helps with the mental game and provides the best means for making the most money.

When I was making markets on the CBOE floor, I would occasionally have lunch with an acquaintance with whom I attended high school. This individual worked for himself, trading his own money. I, on the other hand, traded a firm's money. My arrangement dictated that I had to give up a significant percentage of what I made to the firm. My expenses were a little higher than his as well, as I paid some to the house.

He'd ask me, time to time, why I didn't trade my own money. When he first asked, I didn't have a good answer; I hadn't thought about it. So I began considering the alternatives. At first, I could see the advantages of trading for myself. Why give so much of my hard-earned money to someone else? I was the one making the money. Why shouldn't I keep all of it?

But, the more I thought about it, the more the advantages seemed like disadvantages. Sure. On the one hand, trading for myself would enable me to keep 100 percent of the profits. On the other hand, working for a well-established, *well-capitalized* firm allowed me to trade much bigger than an individual could. I could trade at least 10 times bigger—probably more. I could make more as a firm trader. At the end of the quarter, would I rather have 100 percent of, say, $25,000, or 50 percent of $250,000? The math is pretty clear. *Mama Passarelli didn't raise no stupid kids!*

The psychology of risk is a relevant consideration as well. Trading a firm's money makes it easier to emotionally detach oneself from the monetary impact of each trade. It is easier for a trader to make better decisions when his or her mind is not clouded by emotion—particularly by fear. Of course, firm traders must still keep a tight rein on risk. Losing money means no take-home pay. It could also mean getting let go and losing the opportunity to trade in the same capacity. Though trading for a firm still requires great caution, it is psychologically comforting knowing that there is essentially a put option on your career hedging the worst-case scenario—all you can lose is your job. It's much easier to let the left brain take control when the right brain is at ease.

ZEN, SUPERSTITION, AND THE LONG ROAD OF SUCCESS

There is a Zen to trading. Traders must achieve a certain state of mind in order to be in the moment—to be, if you will, *one with the market*. Call it psychology; call it mysticism; call it the human condition, but one can't trade well without the right attitude. Lack of concentration, lack of confidence, and lack of oneness with the market are the enemies of all traders.

Many—in fact, I'd wager, *most*—traders have rituals and superstitions that help them get in the right frame of mind. I can candidly admit to my own quirky superstitions in my trading ritual. For example, each morning I'd arrive at the train station and would always park in a space in the lot designated with a number that had a 7 in it, or the numbers would add up to, or be a multiple of, 7.

Also, I'd always pick up pennies that were heads up, even in inappropriate or dangerous situations—like in an important meeting, walking in a crowd, or crossing the middle of LaSalle Street on foot.

The right mindset for trading is somewhat unique to the trader, but there are some core commonalities. A positive attitude is essential. If you think you are not going to make money, you won't. An omniscient awareness of the market is important as well. Traders need to see the big picture to find opportunities and avoid red herrings.

They also have to balance patience with adaptability. Sometimes trading is a waiting game. But when things change, traders need to change, or they're left behind. Stubbornness will do a trader in, for sure. Though, sometimes, so can fickleness. There is an art to knowing *when to hold 'em and when to fold 'em.*

I once asked a trader what he thought it takes to be a great trader. He said, "You have to be good at losing money." While this seems a bit counterintuitive, I'm convinced it is the key to longevity as a trader.

Traders will have winners and losers. It is all part of the game. Professional traders will have thousands of winners and thousands of losers over their careers. One of the errors of amateur traders is to focus on the win-loss ratio of their trades. Though this is somewhat important, the real issue is how traders handle each outcome. To be sure, it's even broader than that. Experienced traders think in a more sophisticated way about winning and losing. They think like a casino; they don't think like a gambler.

Consider casino stocks. What industry assignment do analysts give to casino stocks? Not the gambling industry, the *gaming industry.* Sometimes casino companies are even referred to as entertainment companies. Why? Because for most people who go to a casino, that is what they seek—an entertaining game. The fact that money is on the line stimulates right-brained emotional excitement more so than left-brained reason. Gamblers want a thrill; the casino wants its money.

Casinos are categorized as gaming/entertainment because that is the service they provide. But from their perspective, it's all business. They're not looking for a thrill. They're not looking to get rich quick. They're looking for a consistent means of profit—to run a business. They're in it for the long haul.

Gamblers are concerned with each hand of blackjack, each throw of the dice, each spin of the wheel. They hope that any one given play hits it big. Each individual win is a victory. The casino, however, doesn't care much about each individual play. They know that, statistically, they will win some and lose some—lots of each. In fact, they hope to have as many plays as possible, regardless of the fact that they know that they'll have lots of losers as well as winners. Why? Because casinos carefully structure the payout relative to the odds so they maintain a statistical advantage. Each bet has a positive expected return. In the casino business, this is referred to as the house's *edge*.

This is, likewise, the nature of option trading beyond the amateur level. The experienced trader's psyche transcends concerns about individual outcomes and instead focuses on gaining an edge—a statistical advantage—on every trade. Sometimes the expected return on a trade may suggest a small, modest profit. But in trading, as in the casino business, small returns can add up to big profits with volume—both in the frequency in the number of trades and in the size of the trades.

It can be a long road to success for a trader. But, to be fair, it can be much shorter than the road to success in other industries. Success can come fast. And the road can continue on for a long time for shrewd traders. Individual trades do not lead to success. A career is built on the results of the amalgamation of all trades. Success comes from being good at trading, not from having good trades.

KNOW YOUR ENEMY
Market Makers and the Market

Being a trader is somewhat like being a Roman gladiator. Lots of guts. Lots of glory. Lots of risk. Sometimes, when I would come home from a day of trading, my wife would ask me how my day was. More than once my answer was the austere, "I lived to fight another day." As a trader, that's all that one can hope for. The nature of the business of trading is conflict—conflict in perpetuity. It's *Man vs. Market*. And the market is, indeed, a lion of a competitor. Battlers of the market must come prepared. To compete against this relentless foe requires use of a human's most potent weapon: knowledge.

Mainly, traders need to have insight into how the market works, mechanically. They need to have an understanding of the inner workings of what goes on behind the closed doors—metaphorically and literally—in the options business. Before a nonprofessional trader can effectively execute a trade, she or he needs to understand how, in fact, the trade execution process works.

HOW THE OPTIONS MARKET WORKS

Over the past decade or so, the options industry has grown rapidly to be a mechanism of great complexity. Much time, effort, and money has been spent to set up an electronic trading system with integrity, speed, and efficiency that can handle the massive amounts of data necessary to seamlessly facilitate global trading. The system in place today is the product of many people working together, putting in place a dizzying amount of hardware—and backup hardware—and creating troves of new software that can integrate seamlessly with that of brokers, exchanges, clearing firms, traders, and end-user customers.

Though now there is much high-tech infrastructure, the basic concept of how trades are transacted is still essentially the same as it has been for hundreds of years. Underneath the layers of technology, trading mechanics are fairly straightforward.

Option transactions—in listed options—are ultimately consummated on an exchange, of which there are several. Only traders who own or lease trading rights have the privilege to actually execute a trade on an options exchange. Once, only seat holders on a member-owned exchange were granted these privileges. Over the past several years, the ownership structure of many exchanges has moved from the traditional member-owned model to become shareholder-owned entities. On exchanges that are shareholder owned, traders must hold trading permits, which grant them access to execute directly on the exchange, either electronically or (if allowed) in traditional open outcry.

In fact, only a very small percentage of traders have this privilege and trade directly on an exchange. So, how do traders who do not hold a seat or a permit buy and sell options? They trade through a broker.

Customer Order Representation

A broker is a person or entity that executes trades on behalf of another party. Traditionally—before the advent of electronic exchanges and online brokers—there were two different types of brokers involved in executing an option trade for a customer: a retail broker (or institutional broker, depending on the customer) and a floor broker. Today, in some cases, both brokers are still involved in executing an option trade—particularly in the U.S. commodities options realm, where electronic trading has yet to flourish (at the time of this writing). In commodities, the general category of broker may be broadened to include Futures Commission Merchants (FCMs), Introducing Brokers (IBs), Associated Persons (APs), and others.

Most of the time—particularly in the securities options world—the role of retail broker and floor broker has been largely automated. Let's discuss order representation involving the "human touch" first, by examining the different types of brokers. Then we'll look at the way business is typically transacted on an electronic exchange platform.

Brokers

A retail broker is a licensed individual or entity that acts as an intermediary between retail traders and the exchange. Retail brokers are the access point to the exchange for nonmember traders to execute option trades. They act as a liaison of order information from the customer to the trading floor. Retail brokers may solicit customers and give advice on entering and exiting trades. They are paid commission on transactions.

An institutional broker is similar to a retail broker who acts on behalf of individuals. But an institutional broker acts on behalf of larger organizations—that is, institutions. An institutional broker may represent a hedge fund, bank, or any organization that manages money.

The next broker who may be involved in the progression of customer-option execution is the floor broker. A floor broker executes trades on a traditional trading floor by buying from or selling to another trader on behalf of a customer. Floor brokers have trading privileges to execute directly on an exchange.

Getting the Trade to the Pit

Once the order arrives at the exchange, it can be filled either electronically or in open outcry. Open outcry is the long-used system by which traders vocally express bids and offers and likewise consummate trades on a conventional trading floor. If an order is routed to an electronic exchange, a human broker is bypassed and the order is handled by the exchange's automated order-filling system. Let's examine open outcry first.

If the order is to be filled in open outcry, it will be communicated either to a phone clerk or directly to the floor broker. If the retail broker sends the order to a phone clerk, the clerk will create an order ticket and will relay the order to the floor broker in one of three ways: (1) give a written or printed order ticket to a runner to deliver to the broker, (2) "flash" the order to the broker via hand signals, or (3) send the information to the broker electronically. On modern trading floors, runners have mostly been phased out in favor of the other two faster, more efficient means. Faster execution ensures that the customer has a better chance of getting filled at the anticipated price.

There are different types of floor brokers. Some floor brokers stand in a pit—the same pit each day—filling orders for the option classes traded in that pit. And some floor brokers, colloquially referred to as "floating brokers," fill orders in many trading pits on the floor. Floating brokers are called such because they "float" from one pit to the other. Some exchanges—mostly securities option exchanges—have specialists (the CBOE's counterparts to specialists are called Designated Primary Market Makers, or DPMs). Specialists and DPMs act as both market makers and brokers.

Getting the Order Filled

Once the floor broker (or specialist/DPM) receives the order, he or she verbally asks for a market. For example, imagine a retail customer wants to buy five IBM March 120 calls at 2.30. The broker would shout in a clear, loud voice so everyone can hear something like, "IBM, March 120 calls?" or maybe, "IBM, March 120s, what's here?" Notice that the broker does not indicate the price at which the customer is willing to transact, the contract size, or whether the order is a buy or a sell. The broker best represents the customer's order by not *showing his or her hand*.

The other traders in the pit—market makers and other brokers—may respond to the request for a quote. It is more common for a broker to trade with a market maker than another broker. Brokers trade only if they have a resting customer order that can be executed. Market makers are generally eager to take either side of the market (buy or sell) to trade for themselves.

In response to a quote request, market makers state the highest price they are willing to buy (their bid) and the lowest price at which they will sell (their ask); hence, they *make a market*. Typically, market makers trade with great frequency, making many trades a day, and often trading in large volume. Simplistically speaking, market makers hope to profit from the bid-ask spread—that is, buying the bid and selling the offer, capturing the small profits in between. The process of buying bids and selling offers creates liquidity and facilitates trading.

Along with market makers, brokers may respond if they have an order they think may be fillable. Brokers respond with either a bid, an offer, neither, or both, depending on what resting orders they have in their book. Market makers will give a two-sided market consisting of both a bid and an offer, first stating the bid, then the offer.

To the broker's request of "IBM March 120 calls?" the traders in the pit each respond. The broker may get many responses (depending on the number of traders in the pit who trade that option class) of which he or she must take careful note. One broker may, for example, have a resting order to buy at 2.10. This broker would respond "2.10 bid." Another broker might have an order to sell and may say "at 2.35" (Note the word *at* implies that it is an offer to sell.)

Market makers, who are all in competition with one another, are inclined—and sometimes required—to give a narrow two-sided market. Market makers cannot profit if they don't trade. Because only the highest bid and the lowest offer may trade, market makers are incented to give the tightest market they can while still making a profit on the trade.

Market makers are valuation experts in the option classes they trade and know within reason where the market will be. The collective group of market makers will mostly respond with about the same market. One market maker may respond "2.25, 2.35." At the same time another may call out "2.20, at 2.30." Once a best bid or best offer is established, traders in the pit will either match it or better it. Bids below the established best bid are irrelevant, as they won't trade; and offers above the best offer are likewise irrelevant.

The broker listens carefully to hear the market—that is, ascertain the highest bid and lowest offer. Further, he or she must listen to the order in which the highest bid and lowest offer are verbalized. Though this undertaking sounds simple enough, it requires concentration, skill, and practice on the part of the broker.

Imagine hosting a party for 30 six-year-olds. You ask what flavor ice cream everyone wants. This question begets 30 responses shouted all at once. Now imagine that it is essential to get all the kids' orders correct and serve them in the order of their responses! That's about what it's like being a floor broker.

The order of responses to the broker's request is particularly important because if there are two or more responses that are both the highest bid or lowest offer, many exchanges allow the trader who was first to trade as many contracts as he or she wishes. If the broker is wrong about who is first, he'll hear about it—and the trader who was disenfranchised would likely not be very nice about it.

Once the pit responds to the broker in this example, there are two possible outcomes: either the best offer from the pit matches the bid of the broker, which would result in a trade, or the best offer is above the broker's bid and no trade results. A trade is made when a bid matches an offer—that is, someone wants to buy at the same price at which someone else wants to sell.

Recall that the broker in this example is 2.30 bid for five contracts. If a market maker verbalized a 2.30 offer (was "at" 2.30) the broker would look at the trader, say, "I'll buy five," and show via hand signals that he is buying five contracts. At that point, the trade would be consummated—*that's it*.

If the best offer is above the bid, say 2.35, no trade would occur—*yet*. The broker would announce the bid making the order live, or public. In the case where the order is not marketable (i.e., not immediately executable), the broker would say to the pit "2.30

bid for five," or simply, "2.30 for five" (again, when buying, price is always stated before quantity; when selling, quantity is always stated before price). At this point, the order is live and may be executed at any time a trader wants to offer at that price.

Until the order is filled, it is a resting order that is part of the market—public information. Assuming that the best bid from the pit was lower than the broker's bid, the broker's bid will become the market bid. If the market from the pit was 2.25, at 2.35, the broker would announce "2.30 for five." That newly announced bid would then make the market 2.30, at 2.35.

Competing market makers watch resting orders. They each want to be the first to "turn the market" and trade the order—*and beat their competitors*. But they need to wait until the order is worth trading, in terms of value. Specifically, each market maker would watch the underlying instrument, waiting for it to move to a price in which value is created in the resting option order to make it attractive.

For a resting call bid such as the one in the IBM example, traders would eye the underlying asset, waiting for it to decline. A lower price in the underlying asset makes the static call bid more attractive in terms of the call's value relative to the underlying instrument. Because the market maker needs to buy the underlying asset as a hedge against the short call, greater relative value is created when the underlying instrument can be bought more cheaply compared to where the fixed-call bid can be sold.

The traders will wait until the underlying asset reaches the level at which the trade becomes attractive. Specifically, in this example, they wait until they can sell the call above the theoretical value generated by their pricing models. When the underlying asset ticks down to the right price, a trader (perhaps more than one) will shout "sold!" in the direction of the broker representing the order, and make eye contact. At this point, the trade would be completed by this simple verbal acknowledgment.

As an aside, on some exchanges, the word *sold* is always used to consummate trades, whether the trader is buying or selling. On some exchanges, "buy 'em" is used when the trader is buying, and *sold* is reserved, specifically, for when the trader is selling.

Informing the Clearing Firm

After the trade, the two parties to the trade (the buyer and the seller) must send trade information along with counterparty information to their respective clearing firms. This is either done electronically or written on a trading card to be turned in to the clearing firm and manually punched into the firm's system.

The clearing firm needs to know this information:

- Buy or sell
- Quantity
- Option premium
- Which option (class, month, strike, call, or put)
- Time of trade
- Each party's identifying acronym
- Each party's clearing firm

Once each trader communicates trade information, each respective clearing firm processes the trade and adjusts accounts accordingly. The clearing firms then match trade data with each other. Then both clearing firms notify the central clearing firm of their traders' respective buy or sell transaction.

Out Trades

Any mismatch of trade data results in an out trade. Out trades can occur as result of erroneous information accidentally being transmitted by a trader, or from a misunderstanding between the traders about the trade itself. For example, each trader in a trade may think he is buying from the other (with neither thinking he is selling). Or a trader may mistakenly think he is trading with a broker across the pit, when in fact the broker is trading with another trader behind him. In large pits with hundreds of traders, this is a very realistic risk. Any trade criteria can easily be mistaken, especially in an active open outcry pit. Call versus put, wrong prices, wrong quantities, and other culprits all can contribute to an out trade.

Out trades are an occupational hazard. To consummate a trade, they need to be rectified, which often results in a financial detriment to one trading party, or even both trading parties, of the trade. If a broker reports a trade to a customer, the trade is binding as far as the customer is concerned. But, if the broker made the mistake, the broker is financially responsible for any adverse trade adjustments. Market makers have their own set of problems with out trades.

If a market maker has the wrong price, the wrong option, or incorrect information about any other trade criteria, costly ramifications can ensue. For example, imagine a trader who thought he was buying, say, the March 50 calls at 4.00 while a broker with whom he traded thought he was selling, say, the April 55 calls at 4.00. The market maker's rationale for buying these calls (or any option) would have been that they were under his theoretical value. The April 55 calls may or may not have theoretical edge. In fact, if the market maker was the only trader bidding 4.00 on the calls, it is likely a loser.

Hedging is also a potential problem with out trades. Recall that market makers generally hedge option trades by taking a position in the underlying asset. If a market maker made a mistake and needs to adjust the trade, the hedge may be wrong, possibly leading to a financial loss.

For example, a market maker thought he sold calls on the offer and subsequently bought shares of the underlying stock as a hedge. If it turns out that the market maker was mistaken and was actually buying calls, he would need to fix his mistake by changing the call trade to a buy at the offer. First, he'd be trading at an unfavorable price—he'd be buying on the offer. And, he would be mishedged.

To fix the hedge, he'd need to reverse the initial stock hedge trade by selling the stock he bought. But he'd also have to sell more shares to create the correct hedge. He'd have to sell a total of twice the original shares done as a hedge: enough to reverse the initial trade, and enough to hedge the corrected trade.

If the underlying stock has fallen since the initial hedge trade, the trader will negative scalp (i.e., higher buy price than sell price), losing money on the erroneous hedge. And the shares sold to hedge the newly realized long call position that resulted from rectifying the out trade would be sold at a lower, less favorable price.

Sometimes trades need to be nullified as a result of an out trade. If a trader thinks he or she was party to a trade but in fact was not, the trader needs to "bust" the trade, eliminating it altogether.

Busted trades are a hazard for hedge reasons, too. If a trader hedged the trade that needs to be busted, he has to trade out of the hedge, hopefully without too big of a loss.

ELECTRONIC TRADING

Today, with the advent of electronic brokers, there is, arguably, less that can go wrong with a trade, making out-trade risk a fraction of what it was in the past. Electronic trading is more efficient mostly because there are fewer people involved in the trade, and therefore there's less room for human error. Furthermore, with fewer people involved, information can flow faster, making lightning fast execution a thing of the present. And, of course, the execution costs are much smaller too.

Now, in some asset classes (such as securities options), traders can use electronic brokerages that execute electronically at the exchange level. At the time of this writing, there are eight securities options exchanges in the United States. All of these exchanges facilitate electronic option trading. Many of them are exclusively electronic, with no physical trading floor. Trading on an electronic exchange is done in the same manner as described for an open outcry scenario, but it's much faster and much more efficient. There are, however, some new complexities that come into play with electronic trading.

In days past, securities options were "single list," meaning they were listed on only one exchange. Now, most securities options are "multiple list," meaning that the same option class is listed on multiple exchanges. Multiple-list options are standardized with identical contract specifications and so are fungible among the exchanges on which they are listed. Therefore, a trader can buy an option on one exchange and sell it on a different exchange to close the position.

Like the market makers at any one of these exchanges, each exchange is in competition with all others. Each exchange hopes to have orders routed to it from customers. Orders are routed to the exchange that has the best price, ensuring that the customer gets the best fill possible. This incents individual market makers not just to compete against other market makers at their exchange but to compete collectively as an exchange unit against other exchanges.

In electronic trading, there is no human retail broker or floor broker involved. Retail or institutional traders enter trades via their computer into their online broker's trading platform. Once the trade is received by the online broker—which happens in a fraction of a second—the trade is then routed from the broker's servers to the exchange—which also happens in a fraction of a second. The order bypasses the interaction of a human floor broker and executes directly with a trader—probably a market maker—on the exchange. The trader on the other side of the trade gets a notice that he bought from or sold to the broker's customer and subsequently manages the new trade.

Nonprofessional traders are now also exposed to more information as a result of electronic trading. No longer does a broker need to ask the pit for a market and report it back to a customer—a process that once could take more than 10 minutes in years past. Now all (securities options) markets are readily known by anyone with an Internet connection. Markets for all available securities options can be viewed in a layout referred to as an option chain from many online sources, including online brokerages, Google (or Yahoo!) Finance, exchange websites, or other sites catering to option traders.

Professional traders can now automatically generate markets for all the options on which they make markets—which can be thousands. This automation helps not only non-market-making traders get better access to market information but also market makers. It used to be that market makers could trade 10, maybe 20 option classes before the labor of keeping up with their positions and updating their markets became too much to handle. Now the computer does much of the labor involved in a market maker's job. Market makers don't need to be bothered by verbally responding to quote requests; their markets are already disseminated to the world in mass quantities.

In the name of efficiency, there have been many human resources casualties in the option-trading industry. Many trading-floor personnel have had their jobs eliminated by technology. Runners, phone clerks, traders' assistants, and floor brokers are becoming things of the past. Most online brokers still provide for the human touch by having licensed representatives on staff who can interact with customers, answering their questions and discussing individual trades.

Despite the elimination of many jobs in the options industry, there is one role that will always be necessary for facilitation of the trading process—that of the market maker. Though market makers have much of their labor automated, the human decision maker must still act as puppet master to the machines.

MORE ON MARKET MAKERS

Simply put, without market makers, the options market could not function. They are the people with whom the rest of the world trades. When non-market-maker traders buy an option, from whom do they buy it? Usually a market maker. If not for this genus of liquidity provider, traders would have to wait until there was someone else in the world interested in buying from them or selling to them. In some illiquid options, there might not be anyone interested for months. And then, hoping to make the trade at a price both parties find acceptable? Not likely. Without market makers, markets would be so wide that the benefits to hedging or speculating with options would be lost, bringing the options market to a grinding halt.

Market makers stick their necks out in the name of liquidity, buying and selling metaphoric hot potatoes hoping to get rid of them in a hurry. And when they can't? They manage their positions, reduce risk by cleverly hedging positions, and minimize risk all along the way. In providing liquidity to the world, market makers can accumulate huge positions that are not for the fainthearted. But seemingly ironically, market makers are fairly indisposed to risk. They are risk-averse risk managers who make their living herding risk in and out of their inventory of option positions.

RISK AND RISK AVERSION

As the riddle goes: *What's the easiest way to make $1 million trading options? Answer: Start with $2 million.* It's easy to lose money trading options—really easy. So market makers are cautious; they have to be.

They tend to be much more risk conscious than just about any retail trader I've ever met. With the volume they trade, they can't afford to have any loose ends. It's a business; methodical efficiency is essential for success. Car manufacturers don't say, "Ah, there's eight out of ten screws in that door, it ought to hold." Clothiers don't say, "One sleeve is good enough." And professional option traders—in the risk business—likewise don't take on unchecked risk.

As mentioned, one of the most rudimentary techniques used by market makers to control risk is hedging. Each option trade has risk in terms of direction, time, volatility, and interest—each of which is measured by one of the option greeks. This is where market makers focus their attention: minimizing their greeks. They hedge off their greeks' risk. For most trades, direction (delta) is the biggest risk. Fortunately, delta is the easiest risk to abate.

Market makers typically hedge their deltas as soon as they make a trade—within seconds. The easiest way to hedge deltas is by taking an offsetting position in the underlying asset. For example, if a trader is trading equity options, he or she will hedge with the underlying stock. Likewise, a trader trading wheat options will hedge with wheat futures.

Having a delta, positive or negative, means risk. Market makers are experts in risk management, not picking direction. Therefore, they tend to trade *delta neutral*. Delta neutral is when the trader has a delta of zero, or close to it. To get delta neutral, traders trade an offsetting position opposite to the underlying asset in a ratio conforming to the delta of the option trade. So, if a market maker makes an option trade that results in being long, say, 600 deltas, the trader would sell short 600 deltas in the underlying instrument to establish a position with a delta of zero. Traders call this being "flat" delta.

Delta Hedging Example

Imagine a market maker is streaming quotes electronically in Netflix, Inc. (NFLX) options, with the stock trading at $175. An order for, say, 20 of the 185 calls (which have a 0.40 delta in this example) is routed to the exchange to buy at the market maker's offer. The trade executes with the market maker, and he is instantly notified electronically that he sold 20 of these calls.

The market maker quickly calculates the total delta of the position he just established (or it is automatically done for him via his trading software) and finds that he is short a total of 8.00 deltas (0.40 times 20 contracts). That's the equivalent of the directional sensitivity of 800 shares of NFLX. Colloquially, professional equity-option traders tend to refer to this as being short 800 deltas (as opposed to 8.00, or "eight"), moving the decimal point to state the delta considering it is a 100-share-per-contract option.

Again, the market maker is not in the business of taking on directional risk. He must hedge. He immediately buys 800 shares of NFLX to create a delta-neutral trade and eliminate immediate directional risk; for example:

Short 20 NFLX 185 calls	Short 800 deltas
Long 800 shares of NFLX	Long 800 deltas
Net position delta	0 deltas

The trader is flat deltas, but he is not out of all his risk. He still has the option-centric risk that cannot be abated by trading the underlying. He has theta, gamma, vega, and rho risk from the option portion of the trade. To abate risk, the trader has two choices: either buy 20 NFLX 185 calls (and sell 800 shares) to close the whole position and nullify all risk or create a spread by buying NFLX options to minimize—but not totally eliminate—the exposure to the remaining greeks.

The more favorable outcome is to buy to close the 20 contracts on the trader's bid (and sell the stock) to reap a small profit per contract and eliminate all risk. But the more likely outcome is that he will have to create a spread. Why? Market makers are the last stop in the search for liquidity. From whom is the market maker going to buy the calls? Another market maker? Not likely. Not on the bid anyway. The market maker is somewhat at the mercy of customer order flow and must wait until another trader sends an order to sell. And in order to participate in the trade, the market maker must make sure he is electronically disseminating the highest bid too, so that the trade will be made with him and not his competitors.

Market makers work hard to strive to abate risk. They are always looking for trades that enable risk to be spread off. Sometimes, however, market makers must carry positions for some time, particularly in illiquid names. Having eliminated directional exposure, traders are essentially left with a volatility position. Market makers have volatility risk both in terms of gamma/theta and of vega.

Picking Up Nickels in Front of a Steamroller

When market makers have positive gamma, they must worry that the movement is enough to offset the accompanying negative theta. And when they are positive theta, they hope the theta is enough to make up for losses resulting from adverse movement. But in either of these two situations, the payoff that results from the beneficial part of the trade can be expected to be somewhat offset by the detrimental part of the trade.

For example, imagine a short at-the-money call on a $29 stock that has 45 days until expiration and volatility of about 20. This call would have a positive theta of around 0.01. The benefit, or potential profit source, of this trade is theta. The detriment, or potential source for losses, is negative gamma—that is, adverse deltas created from movement in the underlying.

Theta is less than a penny per share per day—only $1 of actual potential profit per 100-share contract as each day passes. If a trader is flat delta, any movement will cause negative gamma to eat into or altogether erase that tiny profit contribution. A trader would have to be short 100 contracts to make $100 per day—if everything goes perfectly. More likely, overall profits would be some fraction of that figure, with some winning days and some losing days.

Therefore, traders must trade in large—very large—volume to profit from their position theta. But, if there is a very big, unexpected move—a Black Swan event, as Nassim Nicholas Taleb would say—in the underlying asset, negative gamma could lead to a huge, disastrous loss. That is why traders sometimes refer to positive theta/negative gamma trading as "picking up nickels in front of a steamroller."

The disproportionate risk-to-reward potential for liquidity providers is easily observable in a negative gamma situation. But for any given position, the risk of carrying a trade can appear to be disproportionate to potential reward—even positive gamma/negative theta trades. If volatility wanes, negative theta can wreak havoc if there is not enough gamma movement to make up for it—particularly over three-day weekends. And big moves in implied volatility can be detrimental as well, while the reward of status quo is modest.

Therefore, it is in the market maker's best interest to hedge, spread, and close positions relentlessly. But because market makers are the terminal liquidity providers, they can't always control the carrying of a position. They just strive to keep positions as small as possible. These traders prefer to profit on the bid-ask spread as opposed to their positions. Market makers are in the business of fighting for nickels and fighting to keep them—not position trading.

7

USING WHAT YOU KNOW ABOUT MARKET MAKERS TO YOUR ADVANTAGE: PART 1

Some of my closest friends to this day are people I met on the trading floor. We share a common bond of personality traits and experiences that are unique only to floor traders. With the emotional highs and lows that come with the package of being a professional trader, one could say that we've been through a lot together.

But when I first met some of these people, it wasn't under friendly terms. *Au contraire.* In fact, I had a very adversarial relationship with many of them at first. Being a market maker is highly competitive. All traders who stand next to each other in a trading pit are in fierce, direct competition.

FRIENDLY COMPETITION

After my first few months trading in the Ford pit, the end-of-year holiday season came upon us. Back in the day, middle to late

December was a great time for parties for people in the trading business. Many of the clearing firms would have lavish parties with big-named music acts, caviar, top-shelf drinks, and incredible attention to detail. Sometimes trading firms would have parties at a remote location with airfare, hotel, and entertainment all comped. In the boom years, this time of year was a blast.

In my first December as a market maker, we were standing around in the pit one day and the topic came up in regard to the Ford-pit Christmas party. This topic was met by some smirks by the longtime Ford-pit denizens. One of the other traders in the pit explained to me how it worked.

The party was to be on the Friday night before Christmas. The trader went on to explain that because there were nine traders in the pit, the party would be at nine different restaurants. We would each pick a place. We could bring our wives; in fact, we could bring whomever we wanted. And we would each pay for our own dinners and those of our guests. The following Monday, then, we would all tell each other about our evenings and how much fun we had—*without each other*.

CAN'T WE ALL GET ALONG?

There was some camaraderie amid our competition. We all stood next to each other in a small, confined area for around seven hours a day. As much as we all wished the others would just go away, we had no choice but to get along. And, to be fair, we were all in the same predicament. When a big order came into the pit to buy or sell, usually everyone participated in the trade to provide the needed liquidity. Therefore, we often all had similar positions. If one person lost money, we probably all did.

And so it was that we competitors all developed a mutual respect for one another. We would talk and tell jokes in downtimes, play games, and ultimately become a tight-knit group. But there was always the underlying, adversarial competition. *There was only so much theoretical edge to go around*. We all wanted the biggest share we could get.

THE ZERO-SUM GAME AND KNOWING WHAT TO FIGHT FOR

In the grand scheme of things, option trading is not a zero-sum game; traders on both sides of the trade can each be winners, they can each be losers, or one trader can win and the other can lose. Therefore, contrary to popular belief, market makers (i.e., the traders on the other side of your trade) are not really in direct competition with the stay-at-home traders executing the position.

If a retail or institutional trader has a disastrous trade, it is not necessarily true that the market maker with whom he or she traded had a windfall profit. In fact, he or she might not have even made any money at all. However, when a customer of the exchange (a retail, institutional, or non-market-making professional trader) executes an order on the exchange, he or she gives up edge to the market. This is the small but important part of the trade for which the market takers must battle the market makers. This is the only part of the trade that is, in fact, a zero-sum game.

Market Maker's Edge

The edge the market maker has is a function of the bid-ask spread. Market takers can't buy the bid and sell the offer. Therefore, each trade involves somewhat of a negative scalp, at least in terms of theoretical value, for non–market makers. Though the trade may be a winner or a loser, nonliquidity providers must buy at a higher price than they can sell. That represents a small loss, or rather a transaction cost, on every trade.

Market makers provide the bulk of liquidity. So the edge given up to the market can be largely managed by considering how market makers price options and subsequently trade. Market makers run theoretical values and buy below theoretical value and sell above theoretical value; hence, trading for what is called "theoretical" (market maker's) edge.

This sort of statistical edge is akin to the edge that casinos have. Though each bet may be a winner or a loser, casinos have a slight statistical advantage on every bet of every game. Market makers, who buy the bid and sell the offer, likewise have a statistical edge—called "theoretical edge" in the market-maker nomenclature. Though each trade made by a market maker may be a winner or a loser, buying the bid and selling the offer provides edge on each trade. Theoretical edge is how market makers make money.

There are several trade execution tactics that non-liquidity-providing traders can use to manage more effectively how much edge is forgone to market makers. These tactics exploit the knowledge of how market makers trade. Following are several techniques for various scenarios, situations, and order designations that retail and institutional traders can use to minimize edge given up to the market.

MARKET ORDERS AND LIMIT ORDERS

Market orders and limit orders are the two basic order types. Market orders are executed at the best available price. Market orders to *buy* execute at the disseminated best *offer*; market orders to *sell* execute at the disseminated best *bid*. Limit orders may only be executed at or better than the stated limit price. Limit orders to *buy* must trade at or *below* the limit bid price and only execute if the market offer is low enough to allow for execution. Limit orders to *sell* must trade at or *above* the trader's limit offer price, if the market bid allows. If a limit order cannot be executed, it will remain intact as a resting order until it can be filled, until it is canceled, or until the end of the day—at which point it expires—whichever comes first.

Limit orders are more commonly used than are market orders—and for good reason. There is some safety in limit orders in that *you know what you're getting*. Conspiracy-theorist retail traders believe that if they send a market order, the broker, the market makers, or both, have some way of changing the market and filling the order at a worse price. This, however, is not a realistic fear, as I can attest.

The Market Order Conspiracy Theory
Neither brokers nor market makers have a means of manipulating the market in a manner that is adverse to the customer (or in any way, for that matter). First, with electronic trading, marketable

orders are not even shown to the market until they execute. When a market order executes, market makers simply get a message that tells them what they just traded. There is no opportunity for market makers to move markets, and no human-broker interaction. Second, in this competitive environment, if one trader lowered his bid or raised his offer to try and get a better trade price, one of his competitors would be there to gladly take the trade on the original market for himself. Third, it's just bad business. Market makers and brokers depend on order flow. Market makers need edge; brokers need commissions. The last thing either of them wants to do is lose a customer's trust.

This conspiracy theory likely exists because sometimes traders send orders to buy at the offer or sell at the bid, and the market happens to move against them right at that very moment. In this scenario, market orders execute at a worse price than expected—on some occasions, a much worse price. While it seems unlikely that the market would *just happen* to move the wrong way when a trader sends an order, it sometimes does. Given the hundreds of thousands of trades that take place each day, it is bound to happen a number of times every day—and it happens to everybody from time to time.

Throughout my long career both as a market maker sending orders and as a retail trader, I've been "victim" to this scenario hundreds of times. It is true, also, that sometimes the market happens to move in the trader's direction at the moment the order is sent, and the trader gets a better-than-expected fill. The way the human mind works is that traders seem to remember the bad fills more than the good fills. Therefore, it seems as if the bad ones happen more, when in reality this may not be the case.

Overcoming Fill-Price Risk

Given the risk that an unexpected market move could result in a worse-than-expected fill, which should a trader use: market orders or limit orders? Generally it is best to use limit orders because the market *can* and *will* have surprise adverse moves. Limit orders provide a level of protection against the unlikely and unexpected. Again, *you know what you're getting*.

But sometimes market orders make sense. When the market is moving very fast, sometimes traders need to get into or out of a position quickly and don't want to miss an opportunity. Market orders can be better in this situation for two reasons. First, market orders may be able to be entered marginally faster because there is one less step in the process: no price. Second, and more important, in fast-moving markets, sometimes knowing that the order will be filled is more important than the price. Market orders are sure to be filled. Limit orders may not execute if the market moves the wrong way, which would lead to a missed opportunity.

Effectively, each of these order types offers its own guarantee and caveat:

- Market orders guarantee a fill, but not a specific price.
- Limit orders guarantee that *if* the order is filled (which is not guaranteed), it will be filled at or better than the limit price.

Marketable Limits

Under certain circumstances, clever traders sometimes use a happy medium: they bid through the offer or offer through the bid. When traders bid through the offer, they enter a higher bid than the current offer. Likewise, when they offer through the bid, they enter a lower offer than the current bid. These limits are entered as worst-case scenarios. Limit orders always trade at the best available price so an order will trade on whatever bid or offer is being disseminated at the moment it arrives at the exchange—even if the order's limit price is worse than the current price.

Bidding through the Offer Example

Imagine a trader, Melanie, is enjoying a healthy profit on calls she bought at 2.00 that are now 6.00 bid. She gets an alert from a news service that is unfavorable to the underlying company and is sure to weigh on the stock price. She notices that, right away, the stock begins to fall. The calls drop to 5.50 bid, then quickly to 5.00 bid. Seeing the market falling, she doesn't want to lose all of her profit. With the calls still 5.00 bid, she enters an order to sell (below the market) at 4.50.

If the bid in these calls holds steady, remaining 5.00 bid, her 4.50 offer will be filled at 5.00. If the bid rises, Melanie will be filled at the new, better bid. If the market continues lower, the order will be filled at the best available bid as long as the calls remain 4.50 bid or better. With the bid above 4.50, the order is essentially a market order. Specifically, it is called a "marketable limit." If, however, the calls fail to be bid below 4.50, the trade will not execute and her order will remain intact for the day or until she cancels it or until the bid rises to 4.50, in which case the order would get filled.

Caveat

Traders on an electronic trading platform should take note that some platforms will warn the trader if he or she enters an order through a bid or offer. Traders may get a pop-up window asking if they are sure they want to trade at that price. Though this is a helpful safety precaution, it can eat up precious time in a time-sensitive situation. Be prepared for this potential snag.

STOP ORDERS

A stop order is an order that can be used to close a position to limit losses, to close a position to protect profits, or to enter a position as a momentum or breakout play. The two basic stops are the (straight) stop and the stop limit, each of which can be either a buy or a sell. A sell stop order is a market order to sell that is triggered if the option trades at (or below) the stop price or is offered at (or below) that price. A sell stop order will have a price below the current market price. A buy stop order is a market order to buy that is triggered if the option trades at (or above) the stop price or is bid at (or above) that price. A buy stop will have a price above the current market price.

Stop limit orders works a little differently. A sell stop limit order is a *limit* order to sell that is triggered if the option trades at (or below) the stop price or is offered at (or below) that price. A sell stop limit order will, like the straight sell stop, have a price below the current market price. Likewise, a buy stop limit order is a *limit* order to buy if the option trades at (or above) the stop price or is bid at (or above) that price. A buy stop limit order will have a price above the current market price.

Limiting Losses

Of the uses for a stop, arguably, the most common is to use it to limit losses. A stop order used for this reason is commonly referred to as a "stop loss." The premise of a stop loss stems from the trading mantra of, "Take your losses fast, and let your profits run." The wisdom in this is that it is generally considered to be a good idea to take small losses when the market moves adversely and let profits continue adding up when the market moves beneficially.

In general, it is better to use a straight stop as opposed to a stop limit to try and curtail losses. If a stop is triggered, it executes immediately at the best price. If a stop limit is triggered, it will not execute until the market reverses course. That thwarts the efforts of the trader who hopes to get out of a trade when the market moves adversely.

Example: Limiting Losses

Imagine a trader buys a call for 9.00. He enters a stop limit to sell at 8.00. Now imagine bad news comes out about the company, and the underlying stock begins to fall rapidly. The call is soon offered at 8.00, triggering the stop limit order. Now the trader has a resting order sell at 8.00 in a falling market. With the call 8.00 offer, the bid would be decidedly below 8.00, possibly much lower, as the market continues to fall. The order will get filled only if the market reverses and begins to rally somewhat and the 8.00 bid is established. But the paradox is that if the stock were moving higher, the trader would likely not want the order to get filled anymore!

With the stop limit, the trader can lose the opportunity to close the position if the underlying asset continues its route. Therefore, the protection that was sought never comes to fruition; *the stop doesn't serve its purpose*. A straight stop is better. If the trader, instead, used a straight stop, when the call reaches 8.00 offer, the sale would have executed on the best bid—perhaps 7.90, perhaps somewhat lower.

When and When Not to Use a Stop Loss

Stop losses are conventional wisdom in many trading circles. Stock and futures traders, for example, are common users of stop losses. The nature of these linear trading instruments is such that their traders potentially have a lot to lose if the market moves sharply against them. Call and put buyers—especially of in-the-money or at-the-money options—likewise benefit greatly from stop losses because of their dominantly linear nature. Though call and put buyers have limited risk compared to stock and futures traders, it is still possible for them to lose 100 percent of the premium invested. Clever option traders further limit losses on this already limited risk trade by using a stop loss.

Call and put sellers may also use stop losses to try to balance out the lousy risk-reward associated with (naked) short options. Limited-reward short-option traders don't have profits that can "run"—at least, not very far. So they certainly don't want losses that can run rampant. Therefore, it is, in many cases, a wise practice for naked option sellers to implement stop losses.

But stops on other types of option plays can be a challenge. In particular, many types of spreads can be poor candidates for stops. Let's take a look at the practicality of stops on a vertical spread.

Vertical Spreads and Stops

Because there are two options involved in a vertical spread trade, the trader gives up edge to the market on two bid-ask spreads—that is, the edge given up is twice that of a single-legged option trade. The double slippage of these spreads can be oppressive in terms of percentage of the potential profit forfeited. This forfeiture can be a big setback in terms of profitability—especially for illiquid option classes. Giving up double edge can also make choosing a reasonable stop price a challenge—for whatever technique traders use to set stop levels.

Example: Vertical Spreads and Stops

Imagine a trader, Darin, buys a 50-55 bull call spread on a somewhat illiquid option class. The market in each option is as follows:

    50 calls: 4.10–4.30
    55 calls: 2.80–3.00

Assume Darin buys the spread at the natural offer. He pays 4.30 for the 50 calls and sells the 55 calls at 2.80, for a net debit of 1.50. The spread has a delta of around 30.

Imagine Darin treats this spread as one would treat a stock in terms of the usage of a stop loss. He enters a stop to sell conservatively about 7 percent below the purchase price of the spread. This trader would likely not be happy with the results.

Seven percent lower than the 1.50 purchase price is about 1.40— just a dime less. If the underlying stock declined just a small amount (just over 30 cents for a 30-delta spread) the spread would be offered at 1.40, triggering the stop. Or if an order came in mid-market on one of these options (to sell the 50 calls or buy the 55 calls), the stop might immediately be triggered as well.

If the stop were triggered, the sale of the spread would execute on the natural bid, which is 1.10. That's about 27 percent below the purchase price of the spread. So much for hoping to be stopped out 7 percent lower! Undoubtedly, the stop trigger was a result of the underlying stock moving lower, and both the bid and offer for the spread would move lower. That means the sale may execute even lower than 1.10. The spread would have a huge, disproportionate percentage loss compared to the small percentage move in the stock. And, in fact, it is a comparatively disproportionate nominal loss (40 cents on the option, *best-case scenario*) compared to the stock (30 cents).

Vertical spreads are low delta (that is, low leverage) option trades. Yet when stops are used, losses can be highly leveraged. That violates the very premise of using a stop loss. The oppressive, leveraged losses on a stop can make its use impractical for vertical spreads.

In order to use a stop on a spread, a concession of a much bigger percent must be accepted, even before the bid-ask spread is taken into account, to avoid the stop being triggered prematurely. A stop level of something like 35 to 50 percent below the purchase price would allow enough room to not get triggered early. That could only be done if there are tight, liquid markets with little slippage afforded to the bid-ask spread after the stop is triggered.

Setting Loss Targets on Spreads Based on Support and Resistance

As well as a fixed percentage stop loss, it is also common for traders to use support and resistance to set stop levels. Because option prices are derived from their underlying instruments, traders would have a two-iteration implementation on their spread stops. Not only do they need to find the level in the underlying asset to set the stop, but they also need to estimate the stop price on the spread based on the potential move in the underlying asset.

Many online brokerage platforms make this task somewhat less complicated by offering the use of contingency orders. Traders can enter an order to sell an option spread if a certain price trades in the underlying instrument. (*Note*: This is a straight order, not a stop order; however, it serves the same purpose as an actual stop and thus must be discussed here.) For traders who want to use support and resistance levels in the underlying instrument to set option loss targets, this is helpful automation. However, this technique is more complicated than it initially appears.

First, there are other factors that contribute to an option's (or option spread's) value aside from the price of the underlying instrument. Traders need to factor in time and volatility changes too. That undertaking can become complicated for setting contingency trades. Traders still need to use the greeks to estimate what price the spread will be trading at given the influences of all three option-pricing metrics (delta, theta, and vega). For even the best traders, this can still be an inexact science.

Example: Loss Targets

For example, imagine a trader, Paul, holding the following long call spread wants to enter a contingency order to sell to close the call spread if the underlying stock falls to a technical support level of, say, $50.35:

50-55 call spread
purchase price: 1.50
Delta: 0.30
Theta: 0.02
Vega: 0.04

In this example, we'll assume that this option class has very tight, liquid markets, making early exits somewhat more practical.

If the stock is currently trading at $52, the stock would have to fall $1.65 to reach its support at $50.35. If the stock, indeed, reached that level, the 30-delta spread would lose about 0.50 in value (that's $1.65 times the 30 delta). Based solely on delta, Paul would enter an order to sell the spread at 1.00, 50 cents lower than where he bought it, to exit the spread when the underlying reaches its support level.

But if that move happened over, say, five days, Paul would also have to factor in five days' worth of theta. With a theta of 0.02, the spread would be 10 cents cheaper, given the same move in the stock. That means that if Paul is using the same support level, he would set an exit level of 0.90 instead.

Traders also need to try to predict implied volatility movements resulting from changes in the underlying instrument. As equity prices fall, one would anticipate volatility rising, and vice versa— but by how much? If this normal inverse relationship occurs at all, it will vary by the individual stock and the individual market scenario. It is difficult to incorporate estimates of volatility changes based on movement in the underlying into setting exit prices (stops or otherwise).

In this example, the adverse move in the stock leading to triggering the sell order is a downward move. Therefore, Paul would need to adjust for the expectation of volatility rising. The stock would be moving toward Paul's long strike, so vega would likely become more positive, contributing even more value (resulting from vega) to the spread. If Paul assumes that implied volatility would rise 3 points, given a stock-price decline to support, he'd anticipate the spread being worth 0.15 more (that's 3 implied volatility points times an estimated 0.05 vega). If the move happened today, his estimated stop price (based solely on delta and vega) would be set at 1.15. If the move happened in five days, his stop price (based on delta, theta, and vega) would be 1.05.

As one can see, estimating an option price based on a move in the underlying instrument can be difficult. The risk is that the trader can estimate incorrectly and have a limit order or a stop order not trigger. As stop orders are mostly rendered useless with vertical spreads, contingency orders are not much better. Sometimes a better alternative is pure trade planning and management in the absence of an attempt to curtail losses by exiting early.

Nuances of Verticals That Affect Stop Decisions

Typical vertical spreads have deltas that are relatively small. For a near-the-money or out-of-the-money spread, a typical delta may be between 0.15 and 0.35. Therefore, the underlying instrument would need to move significantly—between a 6-1 and a 3-1 ratio of underlying movement to option movement—for the value of the spread to change a small amount.

This nuance plays both into how traders select trades and how they manage them. Traders trade spreads based on expectations for the underlying instrument. Because vertical spreads—whether credit or debit—are limited-risk and limited-reward trades, traders initiating verticals don't typically expect very big moves in the underlying instrument. The underlying asset has a fixed range in which the option position will profit or lose. Any further movement becomes no longer beneficial or detrimental. Specifically, with a typical debit spread (starting near-the-money or out-of-the-money), traders expect the underlying asset to move in the direction of their delta to the short strike. And with a typical credit spread (starting near-the-money or out-of-the-money), traders expect the underlying asset to not move beyond the short strike toward losing territory; perhaps they anticipate it to move slightly away from the short strike, farther into maximum profit territory.

If traders expect a big move, they'd likely select a different strategy—not a vertical spread. If the trade is already established and there is a move of significance in the underlying instrument, the trader's original expectations would likely change as the scenario would become different from what the trader originally thought. Still, the price of the spread will change only a fraction of the underlying instrument's price movement.

Vertical Spreads' Time Contingency

Traders need to consider timing as well. With vertical spreads, the time factor is interwoven with direction. Consider a debit spread. If the underlying asset moves to be trading at the short strike or better (i.e., above for a call spread, below for a put spread) at expiration, the maximum profit is earned. But if that move occurs well before expiration, only a fraction of the maximum profit is earned. In the short term, that which is earned is earned largely through delta. Traders must, then, wait for theta to yield the remaining profits for the maximum gain to come to fruition. A similar case can be made for a credit spread. If the underlying asset moves in the direction of delta, small gains are reaped, but theta still needs to do its part.

The same logic applies if the market moves against a vertical spread. If the underlying asset moves to adversely affect the price of a vertical spread, losses will be endured. But those delta losses are only a fraction of the maximum possible loss. Time will contribute to the remaining losses. In either case—debit spread or credit spread—the spread is punished by time decay when it is nearest the long strike. If the underlying is closest to the long strike, the spread will have negative theta. That negative theta will contribute to incremental (daily) time-decay losses.

Stops can only be used to stave off losses resulting from directional movement—that is, delta losses. Therefore, the time factor makes stops less practical for vertical spreads than for other, more delta-dominant plays such as outright option buys or sells. With vertical spreads, when an unexpected move of magnitude happens, the timing of that move matters greatly in how the trader handles the potential loss. A stop or contingency order cannot address the timing issue. Simple tools such as stops so commonplace in linear trading are not well equipped to work on multiprice-influence vehicles such as option spreads.

Stop Limit Orders and Vertical Spreads

Almost counterintuitively, stop limit orders may be marginally better for vertical spreads than straight stops to try and curtail losses, though they are still not ideal. The fact that, in particularly illiquid options, the trader gives up significant slippage when a straight stop is triggered is a deterrent to its use—especially considering that a further adverse move would only contribute marginally to additional losses. Because traders must wait for time to contribute to adding to or erasing losses, it can, in some cases, be better to "work the order" by using a stop limit instead of a stop.

In the case of the stop limit, when the stop is triggered, a resting order to exit the trade is entered that will not immediately trade. This has some advantages with illiquid spreads. First, even if the market rebounds, the bid will likely be far enough away from the offer to not immediately execute stopping out the trade. That often gives the trader some flexibility to cancel the order, if he or she desires to do so. Also, once the stop limit is triggered, it is a resting order observable by the market. Another trader may see the order and take the other side. In this case, the trader goes from market taker to market maker, possibly executing the spread with positive theoretical edge.

Alternatives to a Stop When Trading Verticals

Structuring a vertical spread trade well initially can take the place of a stop loss. Verticals can potentially have beneficial leverage compared to outrights for *small* moves over time. That is, they have comparatively lower premiums but can possibly yield greater returns.

For example, compare the following two trades:

Outright	Debit Spread
Buy 50 call at 4.00	Buy 50-55 call spread at 2.00

Assume the trades are held to expiration and are profitable. If the underlying asset is trading at $55 at expiration, the 50-strike call makes 1.00 (that's 5.00 of intrinsic value minus the 4.00 premium paid). But the call spread makes 3.00 (or 5.00 of intrinsic value minus the 2.00 premium paid). Therefore, traders should look at the initial premium saved on the trade as a sort of built-in stop loss. Compared to the outright, the profits are allowed to run more (though, only up to the point at which the underlying asset reaches the short strike). And losses are taken not faster (because of the time factor), but smaller.

Still, it is not a favorable outcome for a trader to lose the maximum on a trade. Pre-expiration, the theta of verticals acts as its own built-in stop loss. Remember, in an adverse directional move the spread will suffer some delta loss, but theta will then determine whether losses continue or will be incrementally erased by time—depending on the underlying asset's proximity to the short or long strike. This time suspension of losses offers traders an opportunity to either close the trade early without suffering the maximum loss or wait out the trade with expectations of theta offsetting delta losses.

Other Spreads That Don't Benefit from Stops

Other types of spreads involving multiple options require planning in the place of a stop loss as well. Long straddles, long strangles, and time spreads all have diluted delta compared to other option-centric risk. Therefore, stops don't work well with them either. Other trades involving three or more different options give up too much to the bid-ask spread to allow for stops. Condors, butterflies, and complex time spreads—all of which are income trades that have three or more legs—have too much slippage and too much nondelta option-centric risk, rendering stops useless.

USING WHAT YOU KNOW ABOUT MARKET MAKERS TO YOUR ADVANTAGE: PART 2

LEANS AND CANCEL-IF-CLOSE ORDERS

Many limit orders sent to an exchange are not immediately fillable. They remain resting orders to be potentially traded later if the market changes. This phenomenon is very important to the daily role of market makers. Market makers "lean on" these orders, waiting for them to have theoretical edge to trade them. That's what market makers do. Good, experienced market makers remember all the resting orders so they can pull the trigger on them before their competition.

Market Makers and Leans

When it was slow in the trading pit, we would chat to pass the time. I can recall countless times that, seemingly out of nowhere, a trader telling a story, or someone listening to the story, would abruptly interrupt and yell something like, " SOLD ON YOUR MAY 40 CALLS AT TWO AND A HALF!" Then, without skipping a beat, the story would continue as if nothing happened.

Even when it was slow, the most important thing on the trading floor was trading. Traders would constantly interrupt whatever was going on to trade a resting order they were leaning on once it was worth trading. *Multitasking*. In most circles, this behavior would be considered impolite. On the trading floor, that's just the way it was. While trading, or talking, or reading the newspaper, traders always spied the leans like a tiger waiting to pounce.

The Presumed Pick-Off

Once retail (or institutional) traders' orders are filled, they get a confirmation from their broker—with online trading, this can take place in a flash. Getting filled is, of course, the objective of entering an order. But sometimes traders aren't happy when their resting orders get filled. Sometimes traders feel like they get "picked off" by the market makers when the market moves. This is often the case when the underlying asset moves to a point where market makers are willing to fill the order, and it keeps trending after the order is filled.

For example, the market for a call is 4.20 bid, at 4.30. A trader who is long the calls from 2.00 enters an offer to take profits, selling at 4.50, figuring the underlying asset will reach resistance at the point the call is worth 4.50. The trader walks away from his computer. The market begins to tick higher. The calls go 4.30 bid, then 4.40, and finally 4.50 bid, at which point the trade is consummated.

Then, imagine, the trader later returns to find a confirmation of the trade. He looks at the call market to find that it is now 5.50 bid! This is when some traders get buyers' (or in this case, sellers') remorse. Sometimes the trader feels like he got picked off.

Cancel-If-Close Orders

Sometimes, when traders are watching the market move toward their resting order, they can get skittish thinking that the scenario just described might play out and the dreaded "pick-off" will happen to them, causing them to miss out on further profits. Fickle traders will cancel orders as the market approaches their limit price to avoid getting a less-than-perfect fill (i.e., one that isn't selling the absolute top or buying the absolute bottom). Indecisive traders canceling soon-to-be-filled orders is so commonplace that professional traders coined the colloquialism "cancel-if-close orders" to describe an order that will likely cancel if it has a chance of being filled.

The problem with cancel-if-close orders is that sooner or later the market tops (or bottoms) out and reverses course. If traders don't seize opportunities when presented, they can miss them and turn potential winners into losers. If getting an order filled is getting picked off, traders should want to get picked off. *Getting filled is a good thing.*

Traders need to be decisive. Fickleness is a bad quality in a trader. Pick a price and stick with it, for better or for worse. I can recall but a handful of times in my long career where I bought the low of the day or sold the high of the day. It doesn't happen often. And it's not necessary. It's an amateur endeavor. Risking missing out on dollars to make nickels is not a good business model. There is too much risk in that Jenga game for the amount of reward.

FOK and IOC Orders

Furthermore, if traders are genuinely concerned about being picked off, they might be able to pressure the market makers into making a decision. There are two order types that traders may be able to use: fill-or-kill (FOK) orders or immediate-or-cancel (IOC) orders. A fill-or-kill order needs to be either executed immediately in its entirety (i.e., filled) or canceled (i.e., killed). An immediate-or-cancel order must trade either in part or in its entirety, or get canceled. These order types are mostly used by professional traders, but they may be used by retail traders either electronically (if the retail broker allows) or by calling the trade desk and have a representative route the order to the exchange.

With these orders, if market makers are considering taking the trade, they must do so right away, or they will risk losing the opportunity. In this situation, the tables are turned. Instead of the market taker risking a lost opportunity, the market maker must react based on fear of missing out. This tactic doesn't prevent the market from moving to a better price after the trade is consummated. But psychologically, it gives traders the peace of mind that they are not getting picked off, provides a sense of some control, and ensures that market makers aren't hesitating to see if they can get the trade at a better price relative to the underlying asset.

MIDDLING THE MARKET

A common (and sometimes beneficial) tactic for trade entry is "middling the market." Middling the market is when traders enter a limit order between the bid and the ask. For example, if the market is 2.50 bid, at 2.65, a trader may enter an order to sell at 2.55, between the bid and the ask.

The motivation for middling the market is simple: give up less edge to the market. This is a very practical and important tactic that can potentially make a huge difference to the end-of-year bottom line. *Nickels add up.*

Cost Benefit of Middling the Market

In fact, controlling bid-ask costs can be far more beneficial than lowering commission costs, which is the focus of many traders. Often, I talk to traders who hope to save a nickel or two on commissions per contract. For example, a trader may pay, say, 90 cents per contract and would happily drop his current broker flat to pay only 85 cents per contract. Is it worth it? Sure. But, how does this compare to the cost benefit of regularly middling the market?

If the trader could save a nickel in commission over one year on a total of, say, 10,000 contracts, he'd save $500. But if the trader could middle the market successfully on just a *small* percentage of trades, he could save much more. Imagine sometimes a trader middles the market selling a nickel above the bid or buying a nickel below the offer. Other times he gets a better fill by only a penny or two. And sometimes, he simply sells on the bid or buys on the offer without middling. Consider that over time, given the amalgamation of trades resulting in these three outcomes, the trader saves just a penny per trade on average by sometimes middling the market. A penny per equity-option contract is $1 of actual cash. That means the penny saved on 10,000 contracts would save the trader $10,000. The $500 saved on a 5 cents lower commission on that same number of contracts would pale in comparison. Though lower commissions (assuming comparable broker service) are always helpful, the benefits of positive slippage far outweigh the benefits of lower commissions.

But middling the market doesn't always work. In fact, it can backfire if it isn't done correctly. An ill-considered midmarket order can sometimes make a trade much more costly than just trading on the market.

Setting Up Shop

Consider a bid or offer as an advertisement. It's like a sign in the window of a grocery store that says, "Porterhouse Steaks, $6.99/lb." That's the store's offer. If you want to buy steaks, that's what you pay. Certainly, if the offer is attractive enough, customers will come into the store and buy. This is like what traders do when they middle the market; they are advertising a better price to entice another trader to buy from them, or sell to them, as the case may be.

This is what retail, institutional, or prop-trading professional market middlers are doing: they are setting up shop, offering (or bidding) a better price than their competitors. In the instance of a market-middling trade, the trader literally makes a (one-sided) market, providing liquidity in the form of bettering the price—becoming (at that moment in time) somewhat of a market maker.

Risk of Middling the Market

The risk of middling the market is that the market can move away from the limit price, and the opportunity to trade at that price is forgone. For example, the market for a certain call option is 5.00 bid, at 5.20. A trader hopes to buy a dime better than the current offer—saving $10 per contract traded—and enters a 5.10 bid (making the market 5.10 bid, at 5.20). Imagine that shortly after the trader enters the bid, the underlying stock rises. Consequently, the call market rises, becoming 5.10 bid, at 5.30.

What has happened here? At the time the trader placed her 5.10 bid, she gave up the opportunity for a guaranteed 5.20 fill.

In fact, she may have altogether missed the opportunity to pay 5.20. If she wants to be guaranteed a fill now, she must pay 5.30 (and quickly, before the market has a chance to rise again). Or she can, once again, take a chance at a better fill price by middling the market.

Let's say the trader raises her bid to 5.20 to, again, middle the market. Now the trader is taking a waning chance. If the market makers didn't want to trade the midmarket bid before, they likely still don't want to trade it. Remember, market makers are trading for theoretical edge and hedging with the underlying asset, which is moving upward right along with the call. Because they are selling the call, they will have to buy the stock to hedge. With the stock higher, the 5.20 bid is no more attractive than selling the 5.10 bid was when they could buy the stock at a lower price—delta makes sure of that.

Now imagine the market continues to rise (as a result of the underlying stock rising) to become 5.20 bid, at 5.40. The trader can once again raise her bid to middle the market—and risk missing the opportunity to pay 5.40. Or she can pay up and get the trade done at 5.40—20 cents higher than she could have bought it at the outset! In hindsight, the trader in this example should not have attempted to middle the market and should have simply paid the 5.20 offer from the beginning.

Market makers facetiously refer to these thwarted market middlers as "chasers." These overly ambitious traders miss out on opportunity as the market moves away. Then they chase the bid or offer, watching their potential fill price worsen with each tick.

Chasing the market must be avoided. Part of achieving that goal comes down to decisiveness; part of it comes down to know-how. Traders must know the price at which they are content to get filled and make sure they don't miss it. But if traders want to avoid the foolish fate of a chaser, they must also attempt to middle markets only in options that are most conducive to middling. They must enter orders in such a way that they create an amicable agreement between market maker and market taker. The trader must effectively "cut a deal" with the market makers, offering them a smaller theoretical profit for a safer trade.

Market Makers, Risk, and Compensation

The options market is about risk transfer. Market makers take on risk from the public and must be compensated as a result. The more risk a market maker accepts, the more he or she must be "paid" in terms of theoretical edge. This is market making in a nutshell.

Consider one of the riskiest trades for a market maker: a deep in-the-money option on a volatile, illiquid stock. From a cursory look at an option chain, one can infer just how risky market makers must consider these options. The markets are wider than other markets, implying that they must be considered a greater risk. Why are they riskier to liquidity providers? Delta and volatility.

Delta is the biggest immediate risk to any trade made by a market maker. If the market moves against a market maker after he makes a trade but before he can hedge, the market maker stands to lose big. Once hedged, losses—even big ones—are still possible. But potential losses from nondelta option-centric risk are comparatively smaller than delta risk.

Example

Imagine a trader makes the following trade with the following position greeks on a volatile stock that typically has $2 to $4 daily close-to-close net price changes:

	Delta	*Theta*	*Vega*
Buy 100 80-delta puts	Short 8,000	Negative $200/day	Long $500

Certainly the first action of the trader is to buy 8,000 shares of the underlying stock to neutralize the delta. If the assumption is that this is a somewhat volatile stock, it could easily move enough to create a disastrous trade quickly. Just a rise of $1 would cost the trader $8,000 in losses. Even if the stock rose just 25 cents, the trade would lose $2,000. (Note that if the stock fell, the trader would benefit. However, professional traders minimize uncertainty and potential for loss; *they do not take unnecessary chances*. The 8,000 short deltas represent a menacing risk that must be dealt with fast to abate the potential for loss.)

Once the trader buys the shares to hedge, the position consists only of volatility risk. This volatility risk needs to be monitored and managed. The stock must have big enough daily price movements to generate enough profit (from gamma) to cover the $200 a day in theta. And implied volatility changes must remain small. Specifically, the trader would be concerned about implied volatility falling.

Compared to the initial (prehedged) delta risk, the volatility risks are small. It would take 10 days of maximum theta loss (which would assume a grinding halt in stock price movement) to make up for a delta loss resulting from just a 25-cent stock price increase. And it would take a 4-point drop in implied volatility to lose that much as well.

Markets on deep in-the-money options, illiquid options, and options on volatile stocks should be wider because of the assumed delta risk. Again, market makers need to be compensated for greater risk. If the markets on all options were identical, regardless of delta risk, market makers would prefer to trade only small delta risk options. That leads us to our strategy.

What to Middle

There is not much point trying to middle markets on deep in-the-money options. Liquidity providers will likely not give up their risk-compensating edge to trade the order, and there is a good chance of the market taker ending up being a chaser because the option will move more in step with the underlying stock. Logically, smaller-delta options with tight markets on nonvolatile stocks can seem to make excellent middling candidates. However, because of their low delta risk, their markets are typically very tight, with bid-ask spreads sometimes trading one minimum tick wide. For example, at the time of this writing, at-the-money or out-of-the-money options on the Walt Disney Company (DIS) were 1 to 2 cents wide—those are tough to middle.

But spreads are a different story. Because spreads have two options, they have two bid-asks. As discussed, that means traders give up double edge. However, spreads—specifically, vertical spreads (though it is true for some other types as well)—have lower risk. Because vertical spreads consist of one long option and one short option (both calls or both puts), delta, gamma, theta, and vega are all at least partially offset. That presents a potentially unique opportunity for market makers. The two legs in a vertical spread offer two sources for edge on a lower-risk net position. *Win-win*.

But by middling spread markets, savvy traders can somewhat manage edge given up to the market. Maximum edge is given up when traders trade on the "natural" spread market. The natural spread market is traded when a trader buys the offer on one option and sells the bid on the other.

For example, observe the markets of the following spread legs:

May 50 calls 5.00–5.10
May 55 calls 2.40–2.50

The natural spread market, then, is 2.50 bid (or 5.00 minus 2.50), at 2.70 (5.10 minus 2.40).

Trading a spread like this on the natural spread market is *market-maker nirvana*. It's double edge, less delta risk, lower commission (since less stock is traded), and lower nondelta option-centric risk. If a market maker traded either one of these legs on his bid or offer (and then delta hedged), he'd be looking to spread the nondelta option-centric risk.

The market maker would happily take an offsetting position in another option to reduce gamma, theta, and vega. The market maker would gladly trade the other component of the spread shown in the example. But legging the spread has double delta-hedging risk—the trader may miss the hedge on the first trade or the second trade. If the trader trades just the spread, there is only one hedge trade to execute.

And the spread delta is smaller than either of the component leg's deltas, meaning less is lost if the market maker misses the hedge, and commissions are lower. Further, if the trader trades only the first leg of the spread, he has the risk of the uncertainty as to whether or not the opportunity to spread out of the nondelta option-centric risk will present itself. The market maker needs the other side of this trade (or another comparable option with which to create a spread) to reduce risk.

In fact, if a market maker traded just one outright option on the bid or offer, he'd often gladly concede edge on a second leg to establish a lower-risk (spread) position. This is a way to somewhat solidify edge as profit—by hedging the risk. If a public customer presents the opportunity for a market maker to buy one option on the bid or sell one option on the offer and trade the other for fair value, the market maker will often gladly take the trade.

Strategy for Middling

The strategy for middling the market (from the perspective of a non–market maker) is to enter the order in such a way that one can assume the market maker is getting some edge—albeit, as little as possible. Market makers are "paid" in edge. It is the prize for which they fight. They have no incentive to make a trade if there is no edge (or negative edge) in it for them.

Assume that fair value is exactly in the middle of the bid and the ask for any given option. Though this may not always be the case, it is a reasonable assumption. If the theoretical value is in the middle of all options, it will consequently be in the middle of the natural market for any spread that is created by such options.

Traders aspiring to middle a spread order should observe the natural spread market. Then they find the midpoint between the natural bid and the ask. Traders buying the spread hoping to middle the market should bid above the midpoint but below the offer. Middlers selling the spread should offer below the midpoint but above the bid. This concedes some edge to the liquidity providers; thus, it ensures the maximum likelihood of success.

Middling a spread market—as opposed to middling an individual leg—is not just beneficial to the market maker (as discussed); it's also beneficial to the market taker. Traders middling spreads have lower risk of becoming chasers because there is lower delta. Lower "chaser risk" coupled with the prospect of getting filled at a better price means midmarket spread traders reap a double benefit, making a smarter, lower-risk trade. Another *win-win*.

Chicken

When it comes to trading, market makers are not philanthropists; make no mistake about that. Just as the operator of any business would like to make as much profit as possible on every sale—*market makers would like to make as much edge as possible on every trade.* Even if a market maker is presented with a profitable trade (in terms of edge), he may not jump at the chance. He may hold out to see if the trader gives up and hits the bid (or takes the offer).

It's a proverbial game of chicken. The non–market makers want to get filled easily and not start chasing the bid or the offer. Traders get nervous when their resting midmarket order isn't getting filled, and for good reason. They may have to stop playing games and pay up and not miss their opportunity. *Market makers know this.*

But from the market-maker perspective, they don't want to miss their opportunity either. If there is edge in the trade, one of their competitors might beat them to the punch and trade the spread ahead of them. The market might move in such a way that the spread no longer has edge, leading to a missed opportunity.

If the customer is clever, she can punish the market maker for playing games by taking the order away to another exchange. For example, imagine a trader routes an order to the International Securities Exchange (ISE) to sell a put spread with a limit price that is above the bid but below the midmarket point. If the market makers on the ISE don't fill the spread, the trader can cancel it and subsequently route it to, say, the CBOE. It's this sort of maneuver that puts the "negotiating" power in the hands of the retail, institutional, or prop trader and away from the market maker.

The Assumption of Edge

The assumption of edge may not always be accurate. And even if the model indicates edge, a market maker may forgo the trade. One scenario when a market maker may not take a midmarket spread trade that appears to have edge is when he or she already has the trade on that way and would be increasing the position (i.e., increasing risk) by making the trade.

For example, imagine that a market maker who has accumulated large positions over time happens to be long 1,057 May 50 calls and short 1,103 May 55 calls in inventory. The natural market disseminated for this spread is 2.50 bid, at 2.70. An order comes into the market to sell the spread at 2.55. Because the market maker has effectively already accumulated this spread as a result of many previous trades, he's not incentivized to trade it for decreased edge. He'd probably hold out to buy it at the bid. If, however, an order came into the market to *buy* at, say, 2.65, this trader would likely sell for the 5 cents less edge in a heartbeat. Why? Because the sale would result in a reduction of risk—and for edge, to boot.

When the bid and offer sizes are unbalanced (i.e., there's a significantly greater number of contracts on one than the other), it sometimes indicates market makers' preference as to whether they would rather buy or sell midmarket. Think of a trade, buying or selling at the bid price or offer price, respectively, as the bet that a trader is willing to make. Now think of the size of the trade as the monetary value of the bet. Just as a gambler with more conviction on his bet is willing to wager more money, a trader with more conviction on a trade is willing to trade more contracts.

Options and Wagering

For example, imagine a bettor wagers $50, taking the Chicago Bears over the Green Bay Packers, giving 7 points. That means that the Chicago Bears must not only win but win by 7 points in order for the gambler to win. In this example, the team on which the gambler is betting equates to buying or selling. In this situation, the gambler is "buying" the Bears. If he were "selling" the Bears, he'd want the Packers to win.

Seven points is the price he is willing to pay, which equates to the option premium. Certainly he'd rather pay less. If he only "paid" 6 points or 5 points, his chances of winning would be greater. He'd like to pay as little as possible in terms of points. *The fewer points given up, the better the bet.*

Finally, the $50 wager indicates his confidence level at this price and point level. If the bettor were more certain, he'd make a bigger bet, wagering more money. If he were less certain, he'd make a smaller bet. This is the same logic that a trader applies given the size of the trade. A trader who is very confident in a trade will trade more contracts. If he or she views the trade as more speculative, the trader will trade fewer contracts.

There are three important criteria involved in a trade or bet: side, price sensitivity, and size. Let's first consider price sensitivity as it relates to size. If the bettor could instead bet the Bears without giving up any points—meaning as long as the Bears win, he wins the bet—he'd surely make a larger bet than he would if he had to give 7 points on the same game (assuming he's a rational person). Why?

Two reasons. For one (and most obviously), it is a better bet. Giving up zero points is better than giving up 7 points. But, further, in this example, the zero-point bet would have value relative to the market. If everyone else is giving up 7 points to take the Bears and the bettor has the opportunity to "buy them" for even, not only does he have an advantage over others, but he has an arbitrage opportunity. He can take the bet (buying the Bears) for zero points and then bet with someone else taking the Packers (selling the Bears) getting 7 points.

If the gambler makes this pair of trades, he has no risk—only possible reward—that is, arbitrage. If the Bears lose, the gambler breaks even, losing on the bet on which he took the Bears outright and winning on the bet on which he took the Packers with 7 points. If the bears win by less than 7 points, he wins on the outright Bears bet and wins on the Packers-getting-7-points bet. If the Bears win by more than 7 points, he breaks even, winning on the Bears outright and losing on the Packers plus 7.

Note that the price at which one can bet or trade determines which side of the bet or trade the person is willing to take. In this example, because the bettor can take the Bears straight up, he gladly takes the Packers plus 7 (even if he is a die-hard Bears fan). Under some circumstances, the bettor may, in fact, take the Packers even if it is not part of an arbitrage-producing pair of trades. If someone were to want to take (buy) the Bears and give (pay), say, 80 points, even the "Da Bears" Super Fans from the old *Saturday Night Live* skit would take the Packers on that bet. *And they'd bet a lot.* Price sensitivity relates not only to size but also to the side of the bet or trade.

This is exactly how trading works. And it easily translates into the traders' lingo. "I'll pay 7 on the Bears, 50 times" would be a perfectly understandable way for a trader to pose a bet to another trader. Whether gambling or trading, this concept of the intermingling of side, price sensitivity, and size is at the core of the traders' mindset. It is the concept around which all else in trading revolves.

Understanding this mindset gives stay-at-home traders a glimpse into middling markets and inferring what traders want to do by studying bid and offer sizes. It can help indicate whether the big-money traders providing liquidity are long or short and, therefore, whether they prefer to sell or buy, respectively. Undoubtedly, it tells the public which side of the "bet" traders want to take at the current tradable price levels.

Remember, market makers are risk-averse traders who trade direction neutral and ideally prefer not to have a position in volatility, either. If a market maker wants to take a particular side of the trade (buy or sell), it is because he or she has a position and wants to offset it. Hence, if the aggregate bid size is bigger than the aggregate offer size on a given option, one can infer that market makers must be short that strike and need to buy. In this case, they would be more inclined to entertain midmarket offers than bids. Likewise, if the aggregate offer size is bigger than the bid, market makers are trying to sell their longs and are, hence, looking for midmarket bids to trade.

Bid and offer size is easily found in most option-friendly online brokerage platforms. Generally a column can be displayed on the option chain to show bid and ask size information. Again, because market makers trade delta neutral, an unbalanced market would indicate the aggregate market-maker volatility position rather than their directional bias. As such, if the bid size on, say, the October 75 calls outweighs the offer, market makers will likely prefer to buy the October 75 puts as well as the calls because the puts have about the same volatility (gamma, theta, and vega) exposure as the calls, differing only in delta, which will be immediately hedged anyway. In fact, they'd likely be interested in buying any October option with a strike near $75 to create a risk-reducing spread.

USING WHAT YOU KNOW ABOUT MARKET MAKERS TO YOUR ADVANTAGE: PART 3

RESTING ORDERS AND MIDDLING THE MARKET

There is a scenario in which an out-of-balance market indicates something other than market-maker volatility bias. When an institutional or prop trader enters a large limit order between the bid and the ask, it can distort the true liquidity. Experienced traders can spot these orders easily. If there is one option in the chain that has a blatantly disproportionate bid or offer size, it can be a telltale sign of a resting professional order. But traders need to dig a little more deeply to be more certain.

Exchange Breakdown

Traders should consult a breakdown of the bids and offers at each exchange. Many online brokers offer this information. When professional orders are being identified, viewing the markets at each exchange will magnify the disproportionality of size. Why? The aggregate size (of the collective market) in an option chain is, by definition, bigger than any of the component exchanges making up the market in entirety. Therefore, the order will stand out more given the smaller sizes at the individual exchange on which the order rests. Furthermore, resting orders can sometimes be undetectable without looking at the exchange breakdown.

For example, imagine that a particular option class is listed on five exchanges. Now imagine that each exchange is bid and offered for exactly 10 contracts, all at the same price, as shown here:

	Bid Size	Bid-Ask	Ask Size
CBOE	10	0.75–0.85	10
ISE	10	0.75–0.85	10
BATS	10	0.75–0.85	10
NASDAQ OMX PHLX	10	0.75–0.85	10
NYSE ARCA	10	0.75–0.85	10
Market total	**50**	**0.75–0.85**	**50**

Therefore, the market size would be bid for 50 contracts and 50 contracts offered.

Now imagine a professional trader sends in an order to the CBOE to pay 0.80 for 50. The new market breakdown would be:

	Bid Size	Bid-Ask	Ask Size
CBOE	<u>50</u>	<u>0.80</u>–0.85	10
ISE	10	0.75–0.85	10
BATS	10	0.75–0.85	10
NASDAQ OMX PHLX	10	0.75–0.85	10
NYSE ARCA	10	0.75–0.85	10
Market total	**50**	**0.80–0.85**	**50**

Notice that because the market shows only the best bid and offer, only the CBOE's bid is included on the bid side—it is higher than all the others in this example. The aggregate market size is balanced. But it doesn't give an accurate picture of what is going on in the market from a liquidity standpoint. Only upon inspection of the individual exchange markets can one notice the apparent resting order. Certainly, if the professional order were bigger, say 500 contracts, it would be more perceivable and could be spotted even without looking at the exchange breakdown.

To execute against a resting order, traders must look at the exchange breakdown to find where to route the order. For example, consider a scenario in which it is apparent that there is a resting order. A trader notices that there is a profound bid-ask imbalance. There are 500 contracts bid and only 50 offered. The trader happens to want to sell at the bid price of 0.80. If the trader just sends the order via his online broker, the order may be routed to an exchange on which the trader cannot get his entire order filled at 0.80. Consider the following exchange market breakdown for this option:

	Bid Size	Bid-Ask	Ask Size
CBOE	<u>490</u>	<u>0.80</u>–0.85	10
ISE	10	0.80–0.85	10
BATS	10	0.75–0.85	10
NASDAQ OMX PHLX	10	0.75–0.85	10
NYSE ARCA	10	0.75–0.85	10
Market total	**500**	**<u>0.80</u>–0.85**	**50**

If a trader simply enters an order to sell, say, 20 contracts at 0.80, without routing to the CBOE specifically, there is a slight chance that the order may not immediately get filled in its entirety. Why? Though this order should be routed to the exchange with the highest bid—in this case, both the CBOE and the ISE—there is not sufficient size on the ISE in this example to fill the entire 20 lot. Only 10 contracts would execute, leaving the remaining 10 potentially unfilled. Because of competition and each exchange's desire to have volume traded on its own exchange as opposed to another's, whichever exchange to which the order is sent will likely trade the entire order, even if it is fair value. But one can never be sure.

Pick-'em Markets

Sometimes traders on the exchange to which the order was sent have no interest in stepping up to match the other exchange and trade the order. This can result in a "pick-'em market." A pick-'em market is the rare scenario where the bid and the offer are identical. Pick-'em markets are so called because, at that price, traders can pick whether they want to buy or sell. In the last example, if the trader's order was routed to the ISE and only 10 contracts were filled, and the balance of the order (10 contracts) remains as an 0.80 offer on the ISE, a pick-'em market of 0.80 bid, at 0.80, could prevail—0.80 bid on the CBOE, 0.80 offer in the ISE.

Pick-'em markets are rare and short lived. They usually exist only for seconds. In the spirit of filling customer orders, if the exchange to which the order has been sent initially isn't interested in trading the balance at that price, the order will quickly be routed to the exchange showing the executable price.

The risk in this situation is missing opportunity. If, in the brief time it takes to get the order to the correct exchange, the market moves away from the tradable price—in this case, it falls to 0.75 bid (perhaps because a resting 0.80 bid cancels; perhaps because the underlying stock falls and market makers' call bids follow lower)—the trader may miss the chance to èxecute at the desired price. To guard against this risk, traders should always be aware of the exchange breakdown of the bid-ask spread. Traders must route orders to the correct exchange when necessary (for quantity considerations).

EXCHANGE COMPETITION AND THE LIQUIDITY PARADOX

Clever traders can exploit the intense competition among option exchanges. The options industry attracts the fiercely capitalistic. To say competition is intense is quite an understatement. In fact, at the time of this writing—and for several years now—the options market is in many cases more liquid than the underlying market—at least for securities options. Clearly, because the prices of options are derived from the underlying stock, this should not be the case. *But it is.*

For example, consider options on Apple, Inc. (AAPL). At the moment of this writing, the market for shares of AAPL is around 5 cents wide, with small size on the market. Though the market and market size for these active shares change rapidly, there are about 500 shares on both the bid and the offer. The options, however, are tighter and deeper. The front-month at-the-money calls are only about 2 cents wide, with greater than 50 contracts on both the bid and the offer.

Consider that each option represents the rights on 100 shares; this shows a staggering, counterintuitive liquidity paradox. In the derivative market, traders can control 5,000 shares and give up less edge to the market getting in and out of the trade than they can with the actual stock. In the stock, they can only control about 10 percent of what they can by, instead, using options; and traders give up more edge in the process.

To be fair, each call doesn't necessarily have the price sensitivity of 100 shares. But we can account for that by factoring in delta. The just-out-of-the-money calls have a 0.40 delta—indicating that they would change in value 40 percent as much as changes in the underlying shares. Therefore, a call trader can control a position that acts like about 2,000 shares (that's 5,000 times 0.40). Again, this is in comparison to the approximately 500 shares that can be traded of actual AAPL stock.

This is a result of options exchange traders overextending themselves in the spirit of competition. Exchanges are fighting one another for dominance—and, in some cases, for survival. And, to compete with ferocity, traders sometimes take on more risk than they (arguably) should. But, in this case, my enemy's enemy is very much my friend. Exchange competition begets opportunity for everyone else—especially when it comes to middling markets.

A midmarket order presents an opportunity for market makers on a given exchange to trade volume on their exchange instead of letting it go to their competition. These orders are tempting bait. Market makers want the print to go up on their exchange. They'll trade the order unless it represents losing edge or increased risk.

It's becoming more commonplace for clever traders to pit one exchange against another by canceling midmarket orders that don't fill on one exchange and sending them to another exchange until someone bites. This is called "shopping the order around." Market makers monitor such activity closely. They hate to see orders slip away, thereby missing precious opportunity. If there are liquidity providers on any exchange that have the slightest bit of interest in trading an order, they are highly incented to do so, lest they lose it to their competition.

TRADING THE OPENS AND CLOSES

Trading the open or the close involves unique risks not present at other times of the day. These risks affect market makers and non–market makers alike. And the risks affect liquidity. Thus, there is a timing component to liquidity. When the market first opens and on the close, prices can be more sporadic. Let's examine why.

The Open

On the open, bids and offers jockey for position as markets for individual underlying assets equilibrate to find their levels. Trader perceptions and strategies change as a result of overnight news, creating supply and demand, in turn moving stock prices—sometimes significantly. Big moves in underlying assets can result in "gap risk."

Stock prices (and prices on ETFs, indexes, or futures) can open significantly higher or lower than the previous day's trading range, creating a gap on the price chart. Gaps in price action result in delta profits or losses in underlying options.

Furthermore, implied volatility can recalibrate from the previous day's close to the next day's open. Again, this is the result of changes in traders' perceptions and strategies resulting from overnight news. Traders can start the day aggressively buying or selling options to adjust their volatility positions to the new reality of the market. Sometimes aggressive buying or selling can come without warning. Uncertainty of overnight changes in volatility is a serious risk that all traders must revere.

Also, time-decay considerations can sometimes be slightly unpredictable. Traders take the day out of their pricing models at opportune times during the trading day to lower their markets. "Taking the day out" is when traders change the number of days until expiration used in their pricing models to the next day; they move the day ahead. This makes the value of the options one theta increment cheaper, which helps traders to sell long option positions to avoid punishment by erosion of option premium or, conversely, to position themselves to benefit from time decay.

Traders who are trying to aggressively sell want to have the lowest offer among their competitors (and a lower bid, to avoid further accumulation). Therefore, traders are incented to be leaders in taking the day out of their models. But being overly aggressive can lead to selling too many options, resulting in too big a short volatility position. *It is a dance.*

Further, assumptions about interest rates and dividends may change overnight. Political news, foreign stock market advances or declines, foreign currency price action, and foreign and domestic central bank actions all can contribute to recalibrated assumptions about U.S. interest rates. Overnight corporate news can alter traders' expectations of future dividend streams too.

Traders, of course, don't know one another's positions. Therefore, they don't know what changes their liquidity-providing competitors will make to their model inputs (volatility, date, interest rates, or dividend stream). Furthermore, they don't know what retail, institutional, or professional traders will enter into the market in terms of opening option orders. Market makers need to be very cautious. They need to be somewhat noncommittal until the market settles, and they get their bearings in terms of the aforementioned potential pricing changes.

The Close

On the close, similar risks exist. Traders in both underlying assets and in options need to make their final trades before the closing bell rings. On the close, there are a disproportionately high number of orders flooding the market. Gluts of supply or demand can significantly put pressure on prices. All traders need to be cautious of wily price movements on the close.

Furthermore, market makers and other delta-neutral traders need to trade extremely cautiously so they don't miss their hedges. Remember, these traders typically trade a delta-offsetting hedge in the underlying asset following each trade. Each of these hedge trades takes time—albeit, a short amount of time—to execute.

At the end of the day, because there is usually a large number of option orders being traded, there is consequently a large number of stock orders being traded (as hedges). If an option market maker makes a trade in the last minute of the trading day, he or she may not have enough time for the hedge trade to get filled.

Brokers executing option market makers' stock orders along with the glut of other public orders have their hands full. At that point, orders can't always be filled in the same timely manner as usual. Option market makers might get *hung on the trade*—meaning their orders would not get filled. That would mean going home with a delta that's not flat—a cardinal sin for a market maker.

Liquidity providers are best off scaling back on bid-ask sizes in the last minute or so of the trading day to guard against going home long or short deltas. It would be reckless and irresponsible for a market maker to take a big option trade knowing there was a good chance of not being able to hedge. Therefore, option liquidity can wane in the last minute or two of the trading day.

Solution

Try to avoid trading opens and closes. It's always best to trade in high liquidity. The time of day is an important liquidity consideration.

But sometimes traders *must* trade opens or closes. If a trader has a position held overnight and news (favorable or adverse) comes out before the market opens, he or she may need to exit as soon as the market opens to either take opportune profits, curtail disastrous losses, or create a position to exploit an advantageous situation. Trading the volatile and relatively illiquid open is a situational transaction cost to which traders are sometimes subjected. The same situation applies to the close. If news comes out late in the day, traders may need to close positions to take profits or avoid losses resulting from overnight risk or enter a position before the day ends and opportunity runs out. Lack of liquidity is yet another cost of doing business that traders sometimes face.

PRICE SENSITIVITY, LIQUIDITY, AND FEAR

Illiquidity is born out of uncertainty. Intraday, market makers make width and size decisions based on risks of uncertainty. These actions ultimately affect liquidity for the entire market. The risks that market makers battle are measured by the greeks. Understand market makers' greeks exposure and you understand market liquidity.

Risk 1: Delta-Hedging Risk
As discussed, the risk of missing a hedge is among the biggest risks a market maker faces. It is, therefore, paramount to a market maker's decisions on how he or she will provide liquidity. Deep-in-the-money (high-delta) options have wider markets and less size (i.e., lower liquidity). Highly volatile underlying assets also have lower liquidity because of the risk of them moving adversely. Underlying assets that are thinly traded, likewise, have a small bid-ask size in their options.

For example, imagine a market maker buys twenty 50-delta puts. Once the trade is consummated, the trader will need to be able to buy 1,000 shares to hedge. If there are fewer than 1,000 shares at the displayed offer, the trader will not be able to execute the complete hedge. Therefore, cautious options market makers should make decisions about option bid-ask size and depth contingent upon the bid-ask size in the underlying asset.

Risk 2: One-Sided Paper
Market makers refer to orders that come into the market as "paper." When a disproportionately high number of orders are all either buying options or selling options—that is, all on one side of the market—market makers colloquially refer to the orders as "one-sided paper." One-sided paper occurs when, because of events affecting the underlying asset, traders, investors, and hedgers all seek to establish the same or similar positions. This situation can be

the result of favorable or adverse news, technical threshold viola-
tions, recommendations by market-influential traders, or other conditions. For example, if adverse news on a company is released and
the stock price begins to fall, players in the market may be overall
interested in buying puts for hedging and speculating.

Because risk-managing market makers must spread off option-
centric risk, when they buy options, they must sell other options to
spread, and vice versa. But when paper is one sided, they are
unable to do so. Remember, market makers are at the mercy of
order flow. *They don't act; they react.* In order for them to make a
trade, they need the public to send an order to the exchange. If the
public orders are either all buys or all sells, they can't spread off
their option-centric risk. Extreme one-sided paper can profoundly
affect liquidity. Consider price elasticity from the perspective of the
market maker.

Price Elasticity Example

A market maker with no consequential position electronically disseminates a 50-up market in front-month, near-the-money options in
a particular option class. His market, in this example, is 1.00 bid, at
1.10. Imagine that, as a result of a retail trader sending an order to the
exchange, he sells 50 contracts on his offer (1.10). He hedges and
raises his implied volatility to consequently raise both his bid and
ask. Now the market maker is 1.05 bid, at 1.15. He does so because
he'd gladly buy 50 contracts back for a nickel profit and scratch the
stock by trading it at the same price. But he has sold his fill at the
volatility level corresponding to a 1.10 option price tag. He is only
willing to sell more if he is compensated more for adding more risk.

Now imagine that, minutes later with the underlying asset still
trading at the same price, another retail order is routed to the
exchange and executes against the market maker's 1.15 offer. After
having sold another 50 contracts (at the higher price and, therefore,
higher volatility level), he hedges and raises his volatility to dissem-
inate a market of 1.10 bid, at 1.20. He is now short 100 options.

The market maker's price elasticity decisions are based on
reducing risk or achieving a greater average price for accumulating

more risk. By raising his bid to 1.10, the market maker illustrates that he would gladly scratch the first sale—the sale of 50 at 1.10—by buying 50 back at that same level. This would leave him short only 50 options (i.e., less risk) at the higher sale price—1.15. By raising his offer to 1.20, he enables himself to continue to improve the average price of the accumulated position. If he sold another 50 at 1.20, he'd be short a total of 150 contracts at an average price of 1.15.

Imagine that this pattern continues with no other consequential orders executing. All along, the market maker will be raising volatility, not just for that option but also for all options in that expiration month and, perhaps, for near-substitute expiration months, to try to spread off risk. If raising his markets doesn't attract any sell orders, he, all the while, continues getting shorter gamma, longer theta, and shorter vega. He will eventually end up with a precarious volatility position.

After continuing to sell more and more options, the trader would reach a point where he'd have sold so many options (i.e., so much gamma and vega) that the position would become unmanageable. The trader's interest would shift from improving average price to pure risk abatement. His markets would likely become unbalanced with fewer contracts offered than bid. His market may be bid for 50 with 10 offered. The market maker would surely reduce his offer, but he wouldn't want to buy an increased number of contracts at the higher price (and volatility level). Otherwise, he'd negative scalp against his average price—that is, buy at a price higher than the average price at which the options were sold.

This is the mechanics of how one-sided paper affects liquidity. Note that it's not really the market makers affecting liquidity; it's the market as a whole. Market makers are merely the balancers of supply and demand. Market makers simply react rationally to order flow in such a way that they strive to control risk. Once there is too much of an imbalance of order flow, they may shift their psychology and enter survival mode, shedding size commitment from their markets.

Risk 3: Being Married to Illiquid Positions

Sometimes, illiquidity begets illiquidity. There are many stock-option classes (and futures-option classes as well) that, at any given time, are uninteresting to the general public from a trading perspective. They are *out of favor*. In these classes, the options are not actively traded and can sometimes go days, or even weeks, without a single trade occurring. The bid-ask spreads on these markets can be oppressively wide. Why? Market makers run the risk of not being presented with an offsetting trade with which to spread risk. They may be locked into the position knowing they will have to hold it for a long time—*for better or for worse*. Traders refer to this scenario as being "married to" a position.

Traders may have to hold such positions made in seldom-traded option classes for weeks. That, of course, is not the business in which market makers prefer to be involved. Recall that in reacting to order flow and providing liquidity, market makers are taking the opposite side of a position that a position trader has spent a great deal of time analyzing and strategizing. Market makers are, arguably, always taking the wrong side of every position. Being married to a position comes with great danger of volatility, implied or realized. The greater the amount of time a trade is held, the greater the risk.

For this reason, market makers in low-volume option classes must compensate themselves more for the potential "married-to-a-position" risk unique to such options. Usually, low-volume option classes are losing propositions for market makers, as the likelihood of being forced to carry a (unfavorable) position far outweighs the likelihood of profiting by the bid-ask spread. Therefore, few traders make markets in these options, furthering the illiquidity conundrum of these names.

Fast Markets

Fast markets are markets in which extreme market conditions exist. When an option class is in a fast market, its underlying asset is typically highly, and abnormally, volatile. Under fast-market conditions, it is common to see liquidity evaporate. Markets widen—sometimes to the extreme. Often markets that are usually a nickel wide or less can become a dollar wide. Further, bid-ask sizes can become a fraction of the norm for an option class when it enters a fast market.

Traders—both market makers and market takers—must take caution when trading in a fast market. Though the markets are wide, market makers have exponentially more risk in missing their hedge when the underlying asset is experiencing extreme volatility. Market makers widen their markets (and decrease their size) for good reason. In many cases, market makers don't widen their markets enough under fast-market conditions to compensate themselves for the highly increased risk.

The risk for non–market makers is equally extreme. Market-taking, non-liquidity providers, of course, must pay up in terms of the wider bid-ask spread. They effectively pay a low-liquidity premium. Furthermore, they have an increased chance of missing out on getting limit orders filled. A fast market is one of the times that bidding through the offer or offering through the bid makes a great deal of sense.

As an aside, yet another traders' colloquialism has been born as a tribute of sorts to the fast-market condition: the "personal fast market." Often on the trading floor, or in an off-floor trading room, it is common for things to get hectic once in a while. Traders need to be expert multitaskers. They may be dealing with an out trade, watching a stock go against them, and consequently managing the position, making a new trade, looking up a news story to see what is happening in an option class they trade, and more—*all at the same time*. Sometimes traders can get a little wound up when there is too much going on, especially when things are going wrong. It's common to facetiously refer to a trader's frenzied state as a *personal fast market*. For example: "It looks like Joe is in a personal fast market." Or, "I can't talk right now! I'm in a personal fast market!"

10

THE SHIFT OF POWER
How Decimalization, Multiple Listing, and Technology Changed the Rules of the Game

It's good to be king. Or, at least, it was. But, alas! No longer do market makers hold the keys to the kingdom. Those days are gone. The power paradigm has shifted from the hands of the few to the hands of whoever is now clever enough to wield it—*professional and nonprofessional traders alike.*

Indeed, things are different. There have been many changes, both technological and functional in nature. It has been more than a decade of relentless change.

TECHNOLOGICAL CHANGES IN THE OPTIONS INDUSTRY

When I started trading on the floor of the CBOE, I had a CBOE-issued handheld device for analyzing my positions. It was a small but heavy piece of equipment with a black-and-gray LCD touch screen that I could cover in its entirety with my hand. I could see my options and stock inventory; I could see my position delta, theta, and vega for each option class. That was pretty much it. No price charts. No volatility charts. No real breakdown of position analytics. Certainly, no news articles or other media feeds. By today's standards, it was rather archaic.

We had to consult a multitude of sources for the information we needed to trade. There were news terminals with Dow Jones and Reuters news feeds placed sparsely on the floor for members to share. Each pit had a closed-caption television. We had our "sheets"—which is what we called our "morning statements"—printed out each morning with a detailed breakdown of useful analytics that we could reference throughout the day. Though these were static and had to be adjusted by the day's trades, they were helpful.

We who cleared our trades through the firm First Options had what we called "plots," which were profit-and-loss diagrams printed out each morning that showed position risk at some different time horizons up to expiration. Different characters coarsely designated each time snapshot. The risk at one date was shown by a series of asterisks that formed a curve; the risk curve on another date was formed by a series of hyphens; and so on. We traders could pay for additional software tools to analyze our risk. Packages included risk graphs, price and volatility charts, aggregated news, and more. Traders could spend a lot of money on trading aides, if they wanted to.

Today, any option-friendly online retail brokerage firm has analysis software infinitely better than anything I could access when I first started as a trader. Most of what is widely available now simply didn't exist back then. And, best of all, it's usually all in one user interface, and *it's free.*

The retail trader now has the tools professional traders used not 10 years ago and much more. As one would expect, the professional trader's tools have evolved right in tandem. Professional option trading today is very cerebral, which is indicated by its technology.

It was once the case that a bright, aggressive young individual could get a trading job with ease (well . . . *with a little dedication*). Nowadays, many firms looking for traders require them to have a Ph.D. in mathematics and computer-programming expertise. Firms are looking for "quants" to build models that can exploit the market in ways that couldn't have been done before. And seemingly the more models that are built, the more traders compete to build better models. Professional traders are not so much the executors of trades anymore; that function is largely automated. They are the brains that do the programming. *Brains, not brawn.*

FUNCTIONALITY CHANGES IN THE OPTIONS INDUSTRY

Perhaps more important than technological changes are the revampings in the functionality of how the options industry works. Certainly, there have been profound new developments with an echoing effect upon the options business. These changes have greatly benefited retail, institutional, and prop traders, mostly at the expense of the market maker.

Fragmenting the Market

I started my trading career in the epicenter of the options universe. The CBOE was the creator of listed options. The exchange was (and still is) a great innovator within the trading world. It was, at that time, the big fish in the options pond, with just a handful of much smaller competitors. And the CBOE was the physical home of most of the masters of the options universe; the lion's share of liquidity providers—that is, *market makers*—were there.

The CBOE trading floor, where I traded, was segmented into what traders referred to as "pits," designated by posts and stations. Each option class was traded in a specific pit. A pit may have had options on just one underlying instrument (for the bigger ones, such as SPX or OEX), or it may have been home to many option classes.

As mentioned earlier, the pit in which I traded was called the "Ford pit." It was called such because the biggest-name stock whose options were traded in the pit was the Ford Motor Co. I traded Ford options. But I traded options on many other stocks as well, including USA Networks, Carnival Corp., Cox Communications, and Ralston-Purina. Most of the option classes I dealt with at that time were traded only in the Ford pit—nowhere else on the floor; nowhere else in the world. It was mostly a centralized market.

Back then, most options were "single list" options. That meant that, even though there were a handful of U.S. options exchanges, options on some stocks and indexes were listed—and, therefore, tradable—on only one exchange. Some stocks' options at that time were multiple list and were therefore tradable on more than one exchange. But only a relatively small number of option classes were so.

Then, just over 10 years ago, the exchanges began listing what once were single-list options on a number of competing exchanges. Quickly, nearly all options became multiple-list options. The rules of the game changed—and fast. Competition for market makers increased exponentially with ferocious velocity. Not only was a given market maker competing with the 5 or 10 traders standing next to him in a pit at the CBOE but also the cluster of traders on the Philly, the group on the AMEX, and so on, for each option class. This is when the tide began to turn for market makers.

The fragmenting of the options market has had a rippling effect on the options industry. Overall, it has benefited the non–market maker. It has resulted in tighter markets, deeper markets, lower transaction costs, and exchanges constantly working to find new ways to cater to non-market-maker traders—providing more information, faster execution, and more advantageous rules to earn customer business.

This new competition has had some controversial consequences as well. One is payment for order flow—when a trader pays a broker for the first opportunity to trade an order. Another is internalization—when the firm representing the order takes the other side.

One detriment to market makers that was a direct result of the change to multiple listing was in regard to information around closing trades. When options were listed on only one exchange, market makers knew what the public—at least, the big money—needed to do to close a trade. If, say, Goldman Sachs came into the pit and bought 5,000 March 50 calls, the market makers knew its position: they knew Goldman was long 5,000 March 50s. They saw it happen; they saw everything. Most importantly, market makers knew that the firm had to come back to them to sell out their longs and close the position.

Though the firm could exercise the options or let them expire, most professional traders close positions before expiration or roll them to the next month. If the firm wanted out, it had to *come to papa*. It was like sitting at a poker table and knowing what your opponents' cards are.

Now, it is not so. A firm can buy up options on one exchange and in turn sell them out to close on another. The obvious disadvantage to market makers is that they don't know what firms need to do to close if they initiated a trade on another exchange. They don't get to see the whole picture.

Another disadvantage is that there is greater risk of being stuck with an unwanted position unable to spread off risk. In fact, if a firm buys a glut of options on one exchange and sells them out on another to close its position, market makers on *both* exchanges are stuck with open positions with no public trader who needs to come and take the other side. They are saddled with positions that they can have a difficult time exiting; they rely on two-sided paper to balance out positions. Not only was an advantage taken away from market makers, but they have decidedly been given a disadvantage.

In the exchange-competition game the heat has been turned up by the advent of the International Securities Exchange (ISE). The ISE is an all-electronic options exchange—the first of its kind in the United States—that came online in 2000. Backed by big money, it became an instant threat to the once-top-of-the-food-chain CBOE. The CBOE quickly developed a hybrid trading system that allowed for both electronic and traditional open outcry trading. The other U.S. options exchanges also quickly launched electronic trading platforms to compete.

Online Option Brokers

Around the same time as the ISE got underway, online option brokers were establishing their footprints in the business. Brand new brokerage firms were coming onto the scene offering electronic access to the options market. The smart brick-and-mortar brokerage firms knew they needed to compete to survive, and so they too created electronic access to the options market. The firms that weren't as smart and didn't react lost ground in the options business.

Anyone could now enter an order and trade options right from his or her computer. This capability nurtured the largely untapped market for self-directed option traders, making it easy for them to enter trades with the push of a button. In turn, the improvement in electronic trading at the CBOE and other exchanges, along with the innovations of the ISE, helped nurture the online option brokers.

When I first started trading on the CBOE floor, most of my trades (about 90 percent of them) were done in open outcry. The electronic trades were made on the CBOE's Retail Automatic Execution System (RAES). This was an electronic system for distribution of public trades to be traded with market makers who signed up for RAES and agreed to honor the collectively disseminated market. In hindsight, RAES was very archaic in comparison to today's standard of electronic trading. But it was state of the art at the time. When I left the trading floor, up to 90 percent of my trades were made electronically on the CBOE's electronic platform, which was vastly more sophisticated than RAES.

Decimalization

All of this change coincided with yet another major revolution in the industry: decimalization. While options market makers were trying to adapt to multiple listing and electronic trading, the U.S. stock exchanges began trading equities in decimals (i.e., dollars and cents), as opposed to fractions. For years stocks were traded with an eighth of a dollar being the minimum allowable tick size. Soon, all U.S. stocks were traded in decimals.

Decimalization had huge implications. Consider that if the minimum tick size was an eighth of a dollar, the tightest market on 100 shares of a stock could be a minimum of $12.50 wide (or 12$\frac{1}{2}$

cents per share). With decimalization, soon the markets on stocks were tighter—just pennies wide. Today, the market on some highly liquid, low-volatility stocks are a cent wide (or just $1 of edge on 100 shares).

Decimalization in stock prices has been, in many ways, beneficial to the general public and options market makers alike. Tighter markets mean less slippage. But decimalization, in some ways, has changed the liquidity structure of the stock market. It has changed the way liquidity is displayed to the market and how it is absorbed by liquidity providers.

Imagine a stock that typically had a 1,500-up market (1,500 shares on both the bid and offer) that was usually an eighth wide. That basically implies that for assuming the risk of 1,500 shares bought on the bid or sold (short) on the offer, liquidity providers require $12^1/2$ cents per share. Now imagine the shift to trading in pennies. Is it rational to believe that the same stock could be 1,500 up and only be, say, a penny or two wide? Certainly not. The risk premium does not compensate the trader to the same extent. Tighter markets (tighter than $12^1/2$ cents) ensued after the change to decimals, but the market would undoubtedly have smaller bid-ask sizes.

Additionally, sometimes, larger resting public orders can be masked by smaller orders, obscuring true liquidity. For example, imagine there is a resting order to buy 5,000 shares at $74.50. If a $74.51 bid for 100 shares is placed, traders taking a cursory look at the displayed bid size will not have a clear picture of the support that actually exists at $74.50. A simple look at the bid size will show only 100 shares available (though it may be possible to see market depth upon closer inspection).

Decimalization further complicated matters for options market makers when the options market followed suit, moving from fractions to decimals. Options were once traded in sixteenths of a dollar, or "teenies." A sixteenth of a dollar on a single option contract representing 100 shares is equal to $6.25. Once the market moved to decimals, the minimum tick increment was 5 cents. That's $1.25 per contract in edge lost to options market makers (and gained by the public). That's 20 percent of the market makers' edge. That's *real money.* For a market maker who trades, say, 1,000 trades a week, that adds up to a difference—a veritable loss—of around $160,000 a year. (This assumes the trader forgoes half the $1.25 of edge opening the trade and the other half closing it. So, 1,000 contracts times $1.25/2 [or $0.625] times 256 trading days equals $160,000 a year.)

But the violent revolution didn't end there for market makers. In 2007, the Penny Pilot Program was rolled out, allowing a handful of option classes to be traded in penny increments. The first stock was Whole Foods Market, Inc. (WFMI), followed by 12 more in just a matter of weeks. The program has continued, making penny pricing commonplace in the options market. Market makers who thought going from teenies to nickels was rough got a much stronger dose of bad medicine.

IT'S A GOOD TIME TO BE YOU

The end result of this revolution in the options industry has been the empowerment of the self-directed trader. Never before in the history of trading has so much power been placed into the hands of the public. The power has been distributed in a Robin Hood–like fashion from the haves to the have-nots. But it isn't wealth that has been distributed, not directly anyway; it's been the catalysts necessary to gain wealth through trading: powerful trading tools, market access, liquidity, and low transaction costs. Now, only one thing separates the haves and the have-nots in the options-trading world: ability. It is truly a free market.

The fraction of edge that is given up to the market now is nothing compared to what it was a decade ago. Clever traders minimize the edge even further with sound execution techniques and know-how. Slippage is now a small and reasonable transaction cost, instead of a barrier to entry. In fact, occasionally the bid-ask spread represents no cost at all, when a pick-'em market transpires. This occasional single bid-ask price is a result of the cutthroat competition resulting from the decade-plus of industry overhaul.

And it's not just the market makers on the exchanges who strive mercilessly to accommodate the public; it's the exchanges themselves, too. Innovation to create better products to satisfy customer demand is rampant among the options exchanges. New products, such as Weeklys (options that expire around a week after first being listed) and forex (foreign exchange) options are growing rapidly in popularity. And there are expansions in better offerings of current products, such as closer strike prices on many option classes and maker-taker pricing (an exchange model that incentivizes liquidity). All this makes this a great time to be a market taker.

CHAPTER 11

SYNTHETICS AND THE PROFESSIONAL TRADERS' INDIFFERENCE BETWEEN PUTS AND CALLS

"What do you have in the 30 line?" is a common sort of question from market maker to market maker, particularly around expiration. The *30 line*, in this case, is the collective of options—both calls and puts—sharing the 30-strike price in a particular expiration month on a particular underlying asset. Market makers and other arbitrageurs are generally unconcerned about whether an option at a given strike price is a call or a put. Just knowing the net number of options tells the whole story, more or less.

That's because market makers and other volatility-based traders trade differently from the way other traders do. They trade delta neutral. Once their options are hedged, they are left with only the nondelta option-centric risk to manage.

When a call or a put loses its directional characteristic, it becomes functionally similar to the put or call, respectively, that makes up its put-call pair. Puts and calls with the same strike price are synthetically related. Their relationship creates many other synthetic relationships and thus a framework for pricing options off each other. To understand synthetic relationships, one must be familiar with put-call parity.

PUT-CALL PARITY

Put-call parity is a formula that binds together the values of puts and calls on the same underlying asset, in the same expiration cycle, and with the same strike price. The formula for put-call parity for a dividend-paying stock is as follows:

$$Call = Put + Stock - Strike + Interest - Dividend$$

This equation dictates that once moneyness, interest, and expected dividends are factored in, the extrinsic value of the two options in a put-call pair are equal.* The intrinsic portion of an option can be easily neutralized by hedging with the underlying asset and has no volatility component to it. Therefore, if the extrinsic values of the call and put are equal, there is no functional difference between a call and a put, correctly hedged. They are synthetically identical.

SYNTHETIC RELATIONSHIPS

Put-call parity can be extended to postulate several synthetic relationships. Imagine the put-call pair for the Halliburton Co. (HAL) 42 calls with the underlying stock at $41.10. The greeks are as follows:

HAL 42 Put-Call Pair

	42 Call	42 Put
Delta	0.441	−0.559
Gamma	0.088	0.088
Theta	0.023	0.022
Vega	0.053	0.053

---

*Other factors may come into play as well; most important, exercise style. Put-call parity is specific to European options.

Notice the nearly identical greeks, aside from delta. (Slight differences may be noticed if the values are carried out to a greater number of decimal places.) Any small differences are only material in very large positions. For all intents and purposes, one can assume that the nondelta greeks are identical.*

With delta as the only material difference, a trader can cleverly convert a call into a put and vice versa by adding stock to the trade. For example, if a trader bought one 42 call and shorted 100 shares of HAL, she'd have the following position in terms of greeks:

Delta	−0.559
Gamma	+0.088
Theta	+0.022
Vega	+0.53

The negative 0.559 delta value results from the positive 0.441 delta of the long call being combined with the short 1.00 delta of the short stock. Adding stock, however, does not change the gamma, theta, or vega of the trade. Therefore, the resulting position mimics the exposure of a long put. Hence, a relationship can be established:

Long Call *with* Short Stock = Synthetic Long Put

In fact, similar logic can be applied indiscriminately to all the four basic option positions: long call, short call, long put, and short put. The four basic synthetic relationships, then, are as follows:

Long Call *with* Short Stock = Synthetic Long Put
Long Put *with* Long Stock = Synthetic Long Call
Short Call *with* Long Stock = Synthetic Short Put
Short Put *with* Short Stock = Synthetic Short Call

Further, the options in a put call pair can be combined in such a way to result in a position in which the greeks mimic the underlying. If a trader bought one call and sold one put, the resulting exposure would be:

---

*The disparity in theta is mostly a result of interest.

Delta	+1.000
Gamma	+0.000
Theta	−0.001
Vega	+0.000

For all intents and purposes, this is a long stock position. The only difference shown here is a small negative theta value resulting from the initial interest advantage of assuming a long stock position synthetically and thus not committing capital by buying the stock. (Again other greeks are rounded to the thousandths place.)

Likewise, selling the call and buying the put would result in a synthetic short stock position. Therefore:

Synthetic Long Stock = Long Call *with* Short Put
Synthetic Short Stock = Short Call *with* Long Put

It is readily clear that, because of these well-defined relationships, the options' extrinsic values in the put-call pair must be held in line. If the time values of the options in the put-call pair don't balance the equation, an arbitrage opportunity may exist. Arbitrageurs prevent this opportunity from existing for very long.

Other Synthetic Relationships
Relating the value of a put to its call counterpoint (and vice versa) is helpful. But the benefit of synthetic pricing can be taken further. Many synthetic spreads can be created by use of options as well, including synthetic call spreads, put spreads, and straddles.

Synthetic Spreads
In much the same way that a call can be converted to a put, a call spread can be converted to a put spread. In fact, the addition of stock is not necessary to make the leap; only the cognizant understanding of how stock fits into the equation.

A long call spread consists of a long call and a short call with a higher strike price that is in the same expiration cycle. For example a long May 70–80 call spread indicates that a trader is long the May 70 calls and short the May 80 calls. Each call (the long 70 call and the short 80 call) can be converted to a synthetic put—by selling stock against the long call and buying stock against the short call. If each call is converted to a synthetic put by adding the underlying asset, the short stock and long stock offset each other, resulting in a wash trade. Thus, the long call spread is essentially synthetically equivalent to a short synthetic put spread. Indeed, it has nearly identical risk.

For example:

Call Spread versus Synthetic Put Spread

Call Spread with Stock (Wash Trade)	Synthetic Put Spread
Long 1 70 call ⎤ ⎥ ~~Short 100 shares~~ ⎦	Long 1 synth 70 put
=	
Short 1 80 call ⎤ ⎥ ~~Long 100 shares~~ ⎦	Short 1 synth 80 put

Synthetic straddles can be constructed by ratioing the delta hedge. More on this in Chapter 14.

EXERCISE-STYLES CONSIDERATION

American-exercise-style options don't directly adhere as well to put-call parity. When a pricing model conducive to American-style options generates values for calls and puts, the values are mathematically influenced by the possibility of early exercise. It may be desirable to exercise puts or calls that are deep-in-the-money before their expiration date under certain circumstances.

For instance, call options may benefit from early exercise because of dividends. Calls do not entitle their holders to receive a dividend. And market makers short stock against long calls to get delta neutral. Market makers earn a short-stock rebate (interest) on the moneys received when they short stock. Therefore, call holders will exercise calls the day before the ex-dividend date to assume a long position in the stock, if the dividend received is greater than the short stock rebate to be earned on the short stock plus the for-gone time value of the call that results from exercise.

A similar situation exists with puts. But with puts, interest con-siderations can result in their early exercise. Market makers buy stock—and hence pay interest (either actually or in terms of oppor-tunity cost) on the cash used to purchase it—to hedge puts. Deep-in-the-money puts may benefit from being exercised early if the interest to be accrued is greater than the value of the corresponding out-of-the-money call. Why? Instead of holding the long put–long stock combination, traders can exercise the put, thereby selling the long stock that is a cost-of-carry burden. If traders want the expo-sure of the put and stock, they can create the position synthetically by, instead, buying the call for less than they would pay in interest on carrying the stock.

These possibilities are factored into the American-exercise option-pricing model. When there is a great deal of time until expi-ration, these influences can be great, rendering clean put-call parity math impossible. Around expiration, market makers use put-call parity with great fervor because interest doesn't affect values very much. But the concept of put-call parity still reigns, with the effects of early-exercise influences. Synthetic relationships always exist.

USING SYNTHETIC RELATIONSHIPS TO TRADE

Many option market makers use synthetic relationships as a frame-work for making markets—particularly in commodities options, where dividends are not involved and interest is a much smaller consideration. Market making is all about arbitrage. In practice, market makers use synthetic relationships for both call-put arbi-trage and spread arbitrage.

As discussed in previous chapters, market makers opportunis-tically lie in wait for trades. A big part of some traders' methodol-ogy is to wait for put-call parity arbitrage opportunities to arise. A prime example is when there is a midmarket order that presents a synthetic call-versus-put arbitrage opportunity.

For example, imagine the bid on the XYZ August 60 calls is 0.45. Then an offer in the corresponding puts enters the market that enables market makers to buy puts and stock at a price synthetically equal to paying 0.43 in the calls. Market makers could, then, buy puts and stock, and sell the bid on the calls to leg into a conversion essentially for a 2-cent arbitrage profit.

Likewise, it is common for market makers to leg in and out of more complex spreads to attempt to lock in arbitrage profits. For example, traders trade call spreads versus put spreads, sharing the same month and strikes. Because of synthetic relationships, arbitrage opportunities may exist. There are many market makers whose main focus revolves around these arbitrage setups. Specifically, they leg in and out of boxes.

A box is a spread consisting of a long call spread and a long put spread (long box) or a short call spread and a short put spread (short box). In both cases, the options in the boxes share common strikes in the same expiration cycle. For example:

Long Box
Long January 35 calls, short January 40 calls (long call spread)
Short January 35 puts, long January 40 puts (long put spread)

Short Box
Short January 35 calls, long January 40 calls (short call spread)
Long January 35 puts, short January 40 puts (short put spread)

Recall that a long put spread is synthetically equal to a short call spread. If a trader buys both, hence creating a box—for example, buy the 35–40 call spread and buy the 35–40 put spread—the trader is buying the actual call spread and essentially selling the call spread synthetically (almost entirely offsetting the greeks risk). If the prices can be traded in such a way as to lock in an arbitrage profit, opportunistic box traders will trade both spreads, completing the box.

It should be understood that in the long box example, the trader is buying (paying a debit for) both spreads. In the case of the call spread, the trader would buy the higher-valued 35 calls and sell the 40 calls, resulting in a debit, and buy the higher-valued 40 puts and sell the 35 puts. Though both of the spreads are debits, they are synthetically offsetting in terms of their risk. So traders would need to calculate the value of the box to determine if an arbitrage opportunity is present. The theoretical value of a box should be the distance between the two strike prices less interest, factoring in dividend and American-exercise influences.

In practical use, the trader could also consider the trade as two synthetic stock positions, one long and one short. In this example, it would be long synthetic stock in the 35 line and short synthetic stock in the 40 line. This provides a different context for legging, or iteratively combining the components of, the same box spread: it provides more ways to find arbitrage opportunities.

Flat the Strike and Accompanying Risks

A common use of synthetics is to get flat the strike (sometimes referred to as being "converted off") to reduce risk. If a trader is short the same number of puts that he is long in the corresponding call (e.g., short fifty 35-strike puts and long fifty 35-strike calls), the trader is flat the (35) strike. Hedged with stock, all greeks will be nearly zero. This sort of spread gives rise to two synthetic relationships: conversion and reversals:

> Conversion: Short Call *with* Long Put *with* Long Stock
> Reversal: Long Call *with* Short Put *with* Short Stock

Both conversions and reversals are low-risk option strategies. But there will still remain some risks not as clearly identified: interest rate risk, early exercise risk, and pin risk.

Interest Rate Risk

Conversion and reversal values (and all synthetic values) are contingent upon a constant interest rate. When the interest rate changes, the value of conversions and reversals recalibrate. That means that even traders who are flat the strike (i.e., have a conversion or reversal) have interest rate risk. Interest rate risk is identified using rho—the rate of change of an option's value given a change in interest rates.

Early Exercise Risk

If a trader has a conversion, reversal, or a box, the relative flatness of the position is predicated on both options hedging each other's extrinsic value risk. If the short option happens to get assigned while the long option is still in the trader's inventory, the trader will no longer be flat. The trader will have either a synthetic long call or a synthetic long put.

Pin Risk

On expiration, market makers (and, arguably, all traders) have one goal in addition to the everyday goals of making money: avoid *pin risk*. Pin risk is the risk of not knowing whether short options will be assigned. Pin risk occurs when the underlying asset is trading very close to a strike price at expiration and a trader has short contracts in inventory. Even if a trader is flat the strike, there is risk that the short options can get assigned if they are right at-the-money or even, sometimes, slightly out-of-the-money.

Pin risk is a problem because delta-neutral traders need to maintain a delta near zero. If a stock is right at the strike price at expiration, traders don't know whether the person on the other side of the trade (the longs) will exercise or not. So they don't know if their options are to become 100 shares of stock (100 deltas) or zero shares of stock (zero deltas). This uncertainty can potentially saddle an otherwise delta-neutral market maker with a huge delta—that is, huge risk.

Imagine a trader is short 50 of the 35-strike calls, and the bell rings on Expiration Friday with the underlying stock trading right at $35 a share. Do the calls get assigned? Or don't they? Traders hoping to be flat delta need to know, so they know how much stock to have as a hedge.

And what if the underlying stock were to be trading at $34.98, making the calls 2 cents out-of-the-money? The OCC would not automatically exercise these calls. But the trader who owns them might opt to exercise them anyway.

I've exercised slightly out-of-the-money calls many times as a market maker. If I ended the day on Expiration Friday not totally delta neutral, I'd sometimes exercise just enough slightly out-of-the-money calls or puts to get my delta to zero. It is essentially like buying or selling the stock just a couple of cents worse than the market. This is a small cost to minimize the risk of losing big on delta should there be a gap open the following Monday.

Another expiration-day technique to flattening out deltas is to *not* exercise at-the-money options or slightly in-the-money options. This achieves the same results. Instead, here, traders forgo the opportunity to buy or sell at a slight advantage to market prices, with the premise that they'd rather give up a small benefit to reduce overnight (over-the-weekend) delta risk.

Traders also may exercise out-of-the-moneys (or not exercise in-the-moneys) as a result of after-hours news in a stock. Imagine that just following the close on Expiration Friday, a company announces very bullish or bearish news. Traders might opt to exercise slightly out-of-the-money calls or puts, respectively, (or forgo exercising in-the-moneys) to position their deltas for an anticipated gap open Monday morning.

Pin Risk and the Gravitational Pull of Strike Prices

It is generally accepted in the trading and academic communities alike that there is a higher likelihood of a stock closing near a strike price on Expiration Friday than statistics would dictate. Pin risk is, therefore, somewhat of a bigger problem than one might think (than it statistically should be). The gravitational pull of strike prices at expiration is an important statistical circumstance of which clever traders are aware.

However, there exist many amateurish theories surrounding this phenomenon that are, frankly, ridiculous. One theory dictates that it is market manipulators who force stocks to the strike at expiration for some conspiratory reason. Another silly theory is that the market somehow moves to where it causes the "max pain" for certain traders. In fact, the statistical likelihood of options expiring at-the-money is not so sinister or mysterious at all. It simply has to do with market makers trying to avoid delta risk.

When market makers have positive gamma, they frequently hedge with the underlying stock to lock in profits and get back to being delta neutral. This is called "gamma scalping." Gamma, and consequently gamma scalping, is highest on Expiration Friday when stocks are near a strike price on which market makers have long options. In fact, by the end of the day on Expiration Friday, scalping the underlying asset as a result of positive gamma can be intense, as market makers struggle to end the day flat deltas.

Gamma Scalping Example

Imagine a market maker has long options in a particular line near the end of the day on Expiration Friday and the stock is just above the strike price. If the stock moves below the strike, the market maker will need to buy stock to hedge. Why? Because, if the long options are calls, the calls will become out-of-the-money when the stock moves below the strike. Because they will soon expire, any short stock that has been held as a hedge must be bought back. If the long options are puts, they become in-the-money with the stock below the strike. That means that market makers need to buy stock to hedge them because when they are exercised they will result in a short stock position that must be offset. Either way, when the stock moves below the strike, the market maker must buy the stock.

If the stock then moves back up above the strike, the market maker must sell the stock. Why? Long calls would again become in-the-money; the long calls will become long stock, if exercised. So market makers would need short stock to offset the stock. Long puts would become out-of-the-money, presumed to be about to expire. Therefore, long stock that was held to hedge them when they were in-the-money must be sold.

Again, market makers trade delta neutral. They *need* to make these hedge trades just to avoid taking on unnecessary (and irresponsible) risk. Further, their long options are decaying rapidly. They need to gamma scalp a large number of shares just to cover the sky-high theta that comes on Expiration Friday. They need to scalp just to break even.

The supply-and-demand effects of the rather mundane routine of market makers gamma scalping to maintain their positions is what forces stocks statistically toward strike prices. Market makers can have relatively big positions. For example, it was not uncommon for me to scalp back and forth 20,000 or 30,000 shares—sometimes even as many as 50,000 shares of a single stock on an Expiration Friday. And I wasn't alone. I had eight people standing next to me all doing the same thing. All the buying below the strike forces the stock higher. All the selling above the strike forces the stock lower. Ultimately, market-maker hedging of long options makes pinning the strike a self-fulfilling prophecy.

WHAT YOU NEED TO KNOW ABOUT SYNTHETICS

Professional traders exploit discrepancies in synthetics all the time. Aspiring traders must master synthetics. When I was a clerk, one of my mentors would constantly ask things like, "I paid 57 in the put. What's that in the call?" The calculation was second nature to me as a trader. I'd always considered what I did in the call if I made a put trade (or the put if I made a call trade). That's how money is made as a market maker.

Stay-at-home traders, however, don't have the benefit of buying bids and selling offers. It is difficult for them to exploit small synthetic arbitrage opportunities. Still, they must understand these relationships. Synthetic relationships are at the heart of understanding options.

Nonprofessional traders need to understand synthetics for many reasons. For one, it helps them manage trades better. For example, if a trader owns the underlying asset and puts on a one-to-one basis, the trader needs to manage the position like a long call; if a trader finds an out-of-the-money debit call spread to become in-the-money as a result of the underlying asset moving, he needs to manage it like an out-of-the-money credit put spread; and so on.

Traders can set up trades better if they understand synthetics. For example, in many cases a trader would likely do better to establish an iron condor (which is composed of all out-of-the-money options) as opposed to a straight call (or put) condor (which includes some in-the-money and some out-of-the-money options). Given the same strikes, they are synthetically the same, but out-of-the-moneys typically have tighter markets, resulting in less slippage. There may also be margin benefits to taking a synthetically similar position. For example, Reg-T margin requires much more capital to trade a married put (long stock, plus long put) than a long call, even though they are synthetically equal. It is also helpful to understand how liquidity providers think in order to achieve better results on trade execution.

12

EXPIRATION TRADING
Cranking Up the Gain

The world of music was forever changed the day the electric guitar was born. Indeed, music has relentlessly continued to evolve since that instrument's invention. Modern use of the electric guitar allows for a seemingly infinite number of tones and creative sounds. But one of the most recognizable signature sounds of the electric guitar is *distortion*.

Distortion is a guitar effect used in nearly all genres of contemporary music—from classic rock to jazz to heavy metal to easy listening to punk and more. It's caused by overdriving the guitar's signal, producing clipping that, literally, distorts the input signal creating a warm, fuzzy, or even gritty sound (think Jimi Hendrix). Nowadays, most musicians plug their guitars into an "effects pedal" that creates the desired distortion sound.

But distortion was originally discovered naturally—and quite by accident. When the gain on a tube amplifier is turned up too high, it results in the signal being overdriven, causing it to clip, creating a natural distortion of the guitar's signal. It's still the same instrument, still the same musical notes being played, but the sound is profoundly different—more extreme.

Trading options during expiration week is somewhat like playing a guitar with the gain cranked up high on an amplifier. It's the same instrument. But hold on tight and get ready to rock. Options during expiration week are in full overdrive and are much more extreme in how they react to changes in price and the passing of time.

OPTION GREEKS AND THE LIFE CYCLE OF OPTIONS

In order to understand the unique characteristics of options in their final week of life, traders must understand the dynamic changes that option greeks undergo as time passes. Option greeks show a multifaceted snapshot that changes as any of the option price influences change.

Time is one incredibly important price factor that changes the greeks' makeup of option exposure. Time, of course, changes in a uniform, predictable manner. Each day that passes, the option moves a day closer to expiration. Each of the greeks changes as options slowly lose their optionality as expiration draws nearer, because options are moving closer to no longer being options (converting to stock or expiring).

The greeks are an inexact science around expiration. Though theta, gamma, and vega all work conceptually the same when expiration is imminent, their quantifiable utility becomes obscured. Let's consider greeks as expiration approaches conceptually and then study an example.

Theta

In general, options have extrinsic value because of volatility. Options trade and fluctuate in price as a result of the uncertainty of future volatility. However, the fate of options becomes certain at their expiration date, at which point volatility no longer has an effect. Options that are in-the-money at expiration become stock as a result of exercise or assignment; if they are out-of-the-money, they expire. At that point, the value of options based on expected volatility (and the right to exercise) is entirely depleted. This is the nature of time decay, which is measured by theta.

In-the-money, at-the-money, and out-of-the-money options have different characteristics of uncertainty associated with them. Therefore, their thetas are disparate and get more disparate with each passing day. As expiration approaches, the theta for near-the-money options increases. In other words, these options lose their extrinsic value at an accelerating rate. In-the-money and out-of-the-money options lose their extrinsic value at a more constant rate compared to near-the-moneys. Their thetas remain about the same as time passes.

Let's consider time decay from the context of an out-of-the-money option. For example, if a stock is at $30.50 a share (with, say, 45 days until expiration), the 32-strike calls will have some amount of value. Why? Because the stock *might* trade above $32 a share over the next 45 days. It could, in fact, trade much higher.

Perhaps with 45 days until expiration, the value of the 32-strike calls is $0.90. But fast-forward to expiration day and imagine that the stock is still at $30.50. How does the shorter time limitation change the likelihood that the stock will trade above $32 before expiration? The likelihood is drastically less. Why? Simply, there is less time for the move to occur. Consequently, because the opportunity for volatility is less, the value of the option is less. Value becomes less as each day passes.

Similar logic can be applied to in-the-money options. Their extrinsic value is effectively the result of the uncertainty as to their future moneyness or lack thereof. Their intrinsic value changes only by the underlying asset's price changing and is not affected by time. As time passes, the uncertainty about future price movement decreases.

In an example similar to the last one, compare a 29-strike call with 45 days until expiration to a 29 call with 1 day until expiration, both on the same $30.50 stock. Certainly, the in-the-money call with 1 day until expiration has a greater chance of remaining in-the-money. There is not much time for things to change. Extrinsic value is, consequently, less, with less time to expiration: that is, time decay.

At-the-money or near-the-money options have the greatest sensitivity to volatility, and they do so to the very end, as long as they remain near-the-money—and are still in play. They thus have the greatest extrinsic value, and they retain it well. Options that are right at-the-money as expiration is imminent continue to have uncertainty as to whether they will ultimately have (intrinsic) value. Most of the extrinsic value flees the near-the-money option in the final week and definitely at the final day of its life. The rate at which theta increases is exponential and profound during the final week of an option's life cycle and is highest on its last trading day.

Gamma

If theta is affected by time passing, gamma must necessarily be affected as well. After all, theta is the price that traders pay for the benefit of positive gamma, or the stipend they receive for bearing the risk of negative gamma. Just as theta increases greatly for near-the-money options as expiration draws near, so does gamma.

Gamma can be better conceptualized when it is considered in the context of the likelihood of an option expiring in-the-money. Gamma is the rate of change of delta relative to a change in the underlying asset's price. Delta, of course, is the rate of change of an option's value relative to a change in the underlying asset's price. By extension, delta can also be thought of as how much the option acts like the underlying asset. For example, a call with a 25 delta changes in price 25 percent as much as the underlying asset does. But there's another way to look at delta.

Professional traders think of delta as the percent chance of an option expiring in-the-money. Though that is not completely mathematically accurate, it is a useful, loose rule of thumb. Clerks learn this rule from day one.

In fact, the word *delta* is a common term in the esoteric options community lingo that was spoken on the trading floor and is still used by professional traders, even when they are talking about something other than options. Traders and clerks use the concept of delta in everyday conversation to relate the odds of something. *"Hey PAS, what's your delta that Frank is wearing his pink shirt again today?"* Or, *"I'm about 90 delta that my clerk is gonna screw up my lunch order."* Or, *"What do you think the delta is that Steve's parents are first cousins?"* Delta can apply to anything, really. It is one of the many arcane colloquialisms of the professional traders' vernacular.

So, if gamma is the rate of change of delta, by extension gamma can be thought of as the rate of change of the likelihood of an option expiring in-the-money. Of course, time would affect this indicator. Let's revisit the previous example. Consider, again, the 32-strike call on a $30.50 stock. If there are 45 days until expiration, the 32 call might have a 35 delta (i.e., estimated to have a 35 percent chance of expiring in-the-money). But if there were just one day until expiration, the call would have close to a zero delta (almost no chance of expiring in-the-money). Under normal circumstances, the near 5 percent move is not a reasonable magnitude to expect to occur in one day.

Both psychologically and in terms of delta, options essentially get *relatively* more in-the-money or out-of-the-money as time passes—all else held constant. Psychologically, the 32 call doesn't seem far out-of-the-money when there are 45 days until expiration. But with only a few hours until the closing bell, the call would seem very far out-of-the-money. Psychologically, moneyness is relative. Changes in delta (resulting from time passing) parallel the psychology.

As expiration approaches, all deltas (except exactly at-the-money options) increasingly move toward either 100 or zero. To paraphrase: they move toward acting 100 percent like stock (and, of course, if they are in-the-money at expiration, the options will likely be exercised and assigned and will be converted to a stock position) or toward not moving at all with the stock (and if they are out-of-the-money at expiration, they will expire worthless and not be converted to stock).

But at-the-money options remain around a 50 delta, right up through the moment of expiration. At-the-money deltas have the greatest uncertainty of whether the option will become stock or expire—that is, a 50 percent chance (50 delta). The exact price that is the strike price is an important pivot point.

On expiration day, deltas change fast for at-the-moneys as the underlying price moves. Again, at expiration, options will either become stock or not stock (100 delta or 0 delta). Recall that options are automatically exercised (and therefore assigned if they are in-the-money by just 1 penny). So, upon the closing bell, deltas can go from 100, for an option in-the-money by a penny; to 50, if the stock moves 1 penny to be right at-the-money; to zero, if the stock moves another penny to make the option out-of-the-money.

Those last few minutes of the day see at-the-money deltas being most sensitive to changes in the price of the underlying asset. In other words, they have the highest gamma. In fact, as expiration approaches, at-the-money gammas increase with extreme velocity—*just as theta does*.

In-the-money or out-of-the-money options have very small gammas near the time of expiration. Take our 32-strike call, out-of-the-money by $1.50 with 1 day until expiration. If the stock rose or fell 50 cents, the delta would still be around zero—that is, there's no gamma effect, because it doesn't change the likelihood of its moneyness changing very much. But gamma can change drastically during expiration week as the underlying price changes toward or away from being at-the-money.

Again, in this situation relative moneyness is both psychological and mathematical. The gamma for near-the-money options becomes very large as expiration approaches. But in-the-money or out-of-the-money options that are no longer in play have shrinking gammas as their optionality wanes.

Vega

Because volatility loses its relevancy as expiration approaches, vegas naturally get smaller. In fact, the metrics of volatility cannot be used in the final days before expiration. Instead, many traders' measure of extrinsic value shifts to pure dollars and cents over parity, without consideration of vega. Traders who use their models to generate theoretical values in expiration week must raise or lower their implied volatility inputs much more than usual to influence changes in option prices.

For example, with two months until expiration, an option may have a vega of 10 cents. To raise the theoretical value (and consequently bids and asks) a nickel, market makers must raise their volatility input a half a point. That same option, holding all other factors (model inputs) constant, may have a vega of a half of a cent as expiration approaches. To raise the theoretical value a nickel, in this case, the market maker would need to raise volatility 10 points.

Instead, during the last day or two until expiration, traders tend to abandon the model altogether. Time value of in-the-moneys and out-of-the-moneys is zero, and the only strike on which to consider extrinsic value is at-the-money. Instead of using the theoretical value convention (based on volatility), market makers use put-call parity to hold the extrinsic value of the put-call pair (the only two relevant expiring options) in place.

Example: SBC Options on Expiration Day

Several years ago, I was a market maker in SBC Communications (SBC), which is now AT&T Inc. (T). On one somewhat uneventful December expiration day, I traded 25,400 shares (or around $1 million worth) of SBC stock. But I didn't take a directional position. As an options market maker, I was almost never taking a directional position. I only executed stock trades to hedge option trades or to hedge acquired deltas resulting from my position gamma.

I began that expiration day with a very small December position. The stock closed Thursday at $39.75, making 40 the at-the-money strike. The options were traded in $5-strike increments. Therefore, the only December options that were still in play were at the 40 strike, as $35 and $45 were far enough away to lose their relevancy (and consequently extrinsic value). Though I had positions in both in-the-moneys and out-of-the-moneys, they were not relevant to my trading. I was net long only 24 of the 40-strike options to start the day (short 63 calls and long 87 puts). I traded hardly any non-December options that day. Almost all the stock I traded was to flatten out my delta as a result of my start-of-day December options position and December-option day trades.

My Game Plan on Expiration Day:
Hedging Gamma, Day Trading, and Pin Risk

Coming into the day, my plan was, as it was every expiration, to get flat the at-the-money strike. Ideally, I hoped to go home with zero calls and zero puts. Plan B was to go home with only a conversion or reversal at the strike. If the stock was right at the strike at expiration, Plan B wasn't good enough. Short options mean pin risk; long options mean wasted option premiums.

It must be understood that there were two ways, and two ways only, that I was going to close these options: trading with the public or trading with a fellow market maker. Trading with the public was the ideal alternative, because I could buy the bid or sell the offer (i.e., get edge). But, everyone in the pit wanted to close the 40 strike in SBC that day. So it was very competitive. The only way to ensure getting on a broker's ticket was to respond first. All market makers had to have even more awareness than usual on expiration days. On expiration days, it was like they pumped adrenaline through the vents onto the trading floor.

And so it was *hurry up and wait*. We'd wait for orders to come into the pit or trade electronically and hope they were closing transactions. But we would happily add to the position for additional edge. When it comes to getting edge, market makers can't help themselves; *that's what they do*. In fact, that day, I both bought and sold options in the 40 calls and the 40 puts alike. I was reducing options at the strike, or getting edge: *win-win*.

I was legging conversions and reversals all day. If calls were out-of-the-money and I bought a call for, say, 0.10, I'd try to sell a put for more than 0.10 over parity, while hedging. Therefore I'd lock in a reversal for profit. I'd try to do the same with selling calls and buying puts to profit from legging conversions.

But by the end of the day, when there were less than five minutes until the closing bell, we market makers would usually try to trade with other market makers who happened to have the opposite position on. That day, I was short calls and long puts. I, therefore, had on the conversion because I was hedged (i.e., short calls, long puts, long stock). I was looking for another market maker in the pit who had on the reversal (ideally) or a long or short straddle, so we could at least close one side with each other.

The problem is that market makers often have similar positions to one another. If one market maker is long calls, there is a good chance that most others will be long calls too. So the opportunity for market makers to trade with one another isn't always there. When two market makers trade with each other, it is usually for fair value: *neither of them is willing to give up edge to the other*. Offsetting each other's positions is usually the only way trades from market maker to market maker happen.

That December day provided some 40-strike drama. SBC traded above and below $40, making traders anxious about whether we'd get pinned. In the end, SBC closed at $39.30 that day, far enough away to not worry traders about whether we'd get assigned on short 40-strike options—that is, no pin risk. Still, throughout the day, all the veteran market makers worked hard to close the strike.

By the close, I had whittled my 40 line down from short 63 calls and long 87 puts, to short 36 calls and long 39 puts. That outcome was the result of buying and selling mostly smaller trades (10 contracts or fewer per trade), hoping and striving to offset more than to accumulate. There were a couple of larger trades (50 lots).

Option-Day Metamorphosis

On expiration day, a huge metamorphosis took place, as it usually does. On this particular expiration week in December, both the call and the put closed Thursday with 0.15 of extrinsic value. By Friday's closing bell, each option, of course, had zero extrinsic value. That meant theta for that day was 0.15. It didn't matter what our models told us theta should be. Time value started worth 0.15 and was to end 0.00—*that's 15 cents*. Theta couldn't be anything else.

We couldn't take the day out during the day like we normally would. That would, in an instant, take our theoretical values from including 0.15 of time value to parity. We had to manually take premium out of the options by incrementally dropping our bids and offers. Back then, SBC options were traded in nickels. So the out-of-the money options would have changed from 0.10 bid, at 0.20; to 0.05 bid, at 0.15; to no bid, at 0.10; to no bid, at 0.05.

Furthermore, I started the day using a delta to hedge my December option trades (which was partly based on a model, partly estimated); I ended the day considering in-the-moneys to be 1.00 delta and out-of-the-moneys to be zero delta. As I started out net long 24 options, I had positive gamma to start the day. Because the stock traded on both sides of the strike, I was buying stock when it was below the strike and selling stock when it was above the strike. I, theoretically, should have had a decent trading profit in SBC that day, which I did.

The amount of stock I bought or sold to hedge gamma, however, was somewhat arbitrary. If I was estimating delta, I was surely estimating gamma, too. By the end of the day, I was net long only 3 options. Below the strike, I'd need to be long 300 shares against the deltas of the options in the 40 line; above the strike, I'd need to be short 300 shares against those options' deltas. The best thing possible would have been for the stock to oscillate back and forth, above and below the strike. That would have forced me to scalp, just to remain delta neutral.

THE LAST DAY OF TRADING

Theta and gamma make trading during expiration week much different from trading during other eras in the life of an option. Out-of-the-moneys are incredibly cheap, but because of gamma, they can become viable options given a big enough move in the underlying stock. It is a binary outcome: options expire worthless or become stock with 100 deltas that had better be hedged if the trader wants to stay delta neutral.

Volatility and, by extension, vega is irrelevant. Option premium will be zero by the end of the day. It doesn't matter what the volatility level is during the day or how many vegas it takes to raise or lower the option price a given amount. The last day of trading is the one time when volatility just doesn't matter.

Upon expiration, all trades come off the traders' sheets. Money that was made or lost is solidified on all options when they expire. It is an exciting and active time, and it usually is one of the highest-volume days of the month.

13

LIVING ON THE EDGE
Volatility on Every Trade

One of the benefits of beginning one's trading career as a professional is that you have the support of fellow professional traders. Throughout my trading career I and fellow traders would constantly bounce ideas off of one another. This proved to be invaluable in many ways. Indeed, it was a camaraderie that led to honing my expertise as a trader as well as making some great lifelong friendships.

One colleague in particular taught me much of what I now know about technical analysis. But, sadly, his penchant for using technicals turned out to be the bane of his market-making career.

HAVE A HUNCH, BET A BUNCH

One morning before the open, this fellow market maker came up to me looking rather distraught. I asked what the matter was. He explained that he had been analyzing the technicals on a stock in his pit. "It was a perfect setup," he remarked. He went on to explain all the alignments, crossovers, setups, and what-have-yous that warranted the trade.

After listening to the trade-setup details, I asked what happened. He went on to tell me that he bought a few hundred calls, *unhedged*.

"And then?" I inquired.

"You wouldn't believe it. The stock rose 10 bucks, just like I thought it would!" he said. "I made $250,000 yesterday on a gap opening."

"So, what's the problem?" I asked.

His reply: "Bob [our risk manager] said if I ever do that again, he's going to fire me!"

What Bob (and all experienced risk professionals) knew was that market makers are not in the business of guessing the right direction with speculative directional plays, or "delta bets." They are primarily in the business of statistical arbitrage, and secondly, in the business of volatility trading. But they are decidedly *not* in the business of directional trading.

Everyone likes a nice windfall profit, and $250,000 in an instant is nothing to sneeze at. But a speculative trade such as the one just mentioned could have just as easily gone the other way. Alas, *if the hunch is wrong, the bunch is gone.*

VOLATILITY: THE REAL COMMODITY

As an options market maker, the problem with delta bets is that delta is generally a much bigger risk than the risks associated with volatility. Furthermore, it is difficult—some academics would argue that it is impossible—to accurately predict the direction of a stock with any degree of statistical significance. Volatility, on the other hand, is arguably much more predictable. For example, the pattern of volatility rising as earnings approach and falling after the announcement can often be systematically observed in many option classes *like clockwork.*

Market makers hedge option trades to eliminate the haphazard directional risk in favor of being left with only the two volatility risks of vega (implied volatility) and gamma/theta (realized volatility). In fact, market makers would generally prefer to also eliminate volatility risk in favor of the arbitrage-like scenario of buying bids and selling offers and going home flat each night. However, positions usually cannot be completely eliminated because each individual option is not liquid enough to day trade and end each day with no position in any series. Thus options must be spread to reduce the impact of vega, gamma, and theta.

This framework for systematic risk abatement can only be possible if traders use the framework of volatility to trade options of the same class in a manner that pits the volatility risk of one option against another within the same class. Volatility is the commonality that relates all options in a particular class together to be essentially a single tradable commodity.

Models, Theoreticals, Spreading, and Edge

If two options are identical in every way except for, say, their strike prices or their expiration months, it is mathematically possible to find the value of one option based on the value of the other with the help of an option-pricing model. Option-pricing models calculate option values based on valuation inputs, such as price of the underlying asset, time to expiration, interest, and volatility.

Let's start with the assumption that the only discernable difference between two particular options is strike price (assume all other pricing inputs are the same). For this, we'd use an option-pricing calculator to generate theoretical values for each option. Start by modeling the first option so that the theoretical value lines up between its bid-ask spread. Then change only the strike-price input in the calculation to yield the value of a comparable option with a different strike. The same can be said about changing the expiration month and keeping all else constant.

Because the value of one option can be derived from the value of another option, arbitrageurs can exploit opportunities when option values are out of line with the theoretical values generated by models. This value exploitation is accomplished through spreading. Let's look at a basic example.

Basic Example*

Imagine, for a particular option series, the 65-strike call is 2.30 bid at 2.40. Therefore, a trader would enter inputs into an option-pricing calculator to yield a theoretical value of 2.35—right in the middle of the bid and the offer. In this example, the required inputs to yield such a value would be:

Stock px: $65
Strike: 65
Days: 46
Interest: 1%
Dividends: n/a
Volatility: 25

In this example, to calculate the value of another option in the same option class, the trader needs only to change a single value in the model. To find the value of the 70-strike call based on constant inputs, the trader would change only the strike. Thus, the inputs would be:

Stock px: $65
Strike: **70**
Days: 46
Interest: 1%
Dividends: n/a
Volatility: 25

These inputs used for the 70-strike call—all identical to the inputs used for the 65 call except, of course, the strike—would, in this case, yield a theoretical value of 0.70.

From this technique, traders can use relative option prices to create spreads for the purpose of finding value trades. In this case, the modeled value of the spread is 1.65 (2.35 minus 0.70).

Imagine an opportunity arises in which the 65 calls are offered midmarket at their theoretical value of 2.35 and the 70 calls are 0.75

---

*Assume that there is no volatility skew.

bid. A trader can leg into the spread for positive theoretical value, or edge, by buying the 65 calls and selling the 70 calls. The legged trade would then be:

	Trade	Value
(Buy) 65 calls at	2.35	2.35
(Sell) 70 calls at	0.75	0.70
Spread	1.60 (debit)	1.65

Because the spread is valued at 1.65, the trader reaps a theoretical profit of 5 cents per contract. In addition to locking in the spread at an advantageous price, the trader also achieves the goal of reducing risk, as the spread has less risk than either of the two legs outright.

This simple example has been a very "retail view" of how this process works. But it is not far off from the reality of how trading works in the market-maker paradigm. The major differences are model interfacing and volatility skews.

Market Maker Pricing, Edge, and Sheets

Retail traders arguably have time to use basic option calculators to generate the theoretical value of one option at a time, but market makers and other active professionals do not. Market makers must watch (either individually or in an automated fashion) the markets of all options they trade. And because they are in direct competition with one another, they need to be able to access the information fast. Thus, traders must pregenerate the theoretical values in advance so that they can be referenced quickly and easily.

The more archaic, and somewhat dated, way of preparing such information was for traders to run "trading sheets," or simply "sheets," every morning before the open. Trading sheets were sheets of paper—letter or legal size—full of matrices of option values, usually with the strike prices running up and down and the varying price of the underlying asset running across.

Table 13.1 is typical of the layout of a market maker's trading sheets. In general, calls are on one side (shown here to the left of

Table 13.1
Sample Market Maker's Trading Sheet

	41.00	41.50	42.00	42.50
30	11.06–0.00	11.56–0.00	12.06–0.00	12.56–0.00
35	6.22–0.15	6.69–0.12	7.1–0.09	7.64–0.07
40	2.40–1.31	2.74–1.14	3.05–0.97	3.41–0.83
45	0.54–4.45	0.66–4.07	0.80–3.70	0.95–3.36
50	0.07–8.97	0.09–8.49	0.11–8.02	0.13–7.56

each dash) and puts on the other (shown on the right). For example, with the underlying stock at $41.50, the 45 calls would be worth 0.66 and the puts would be worth 4.07.

This is but a simplified example of the types of trading sheets that traders would actually use. What else might be on the sheets? First, there would be more information. Typically, the delta of each option would be included, often shown in a smaller font below each theoretical value. And commonly there would be other information, including greeks for each strike, and spread calculations. Options at each strike would be run at its unique volatility level to account for vertical skew. The volatility information per strike would likely also be shown.

There would be more prices too. A complete set of sheets would have several dollars of underlying prices higher and lower than the previous day's close to account for possible price movements throughout the trading day. Data for all the strikes available to trade on the option class would also appear. Also, a different set of sheets would be used for each trading month. All this would account for clerks running pages and pages of these matrices for their traders to use during market hours. And if volatility changed or when option value changed by theta coming out of the options intraday, the clerks would have to scrap the old sheets and run a whole new set.

The objective is to buy below theoretical value and sell above it. As open outcry trading would go, a broker would ask for a market, and market makers would consequently respond with a bid and an ask to buy below or sell above their "sheets," or theoretical values.

For example, a broker might call out "May 40 calls. What's here?" Then all the competing market makers would see where the underlying is trading, then look down the column that corresponds with the underlying stock price (adjusting for delta, if the stock is not exactly at the 50-cent mark) to the row in which the 40-strike calls are displayed. In this case, with the stock trading at $41 a share, the 40 calls are theoretically worth 2.40. A trader might make the market 2.35 bid, at 2.45.

Nowadays, with the advent of featherweight, touch-screen laptops and tablet computers, traders generally carry a computer instead of trading sheets to show the matrices of option values. Computers have the advantage of automatically updating option values as the underlying stock price changes. And, traders can change their values to reflect changes in volatility, skew slopes, days to expiration, and more without having to run new sheets. Some applications calculate complex spreads for traders faster than would be possible manually.

Trading Dynamic Volatility

Paper sheets or electronic sheets, spreads or outrights—the name of the game is always to buy below theoretical values and sell above them. But theoretical values are contingent upon a fixed volatility value. The problem is that volatility is not fixed. It dynamically changes with supply and demand. When volatility changes, traders must raise or lower their volatility assumption to reflect market conditions.

Volatility Trade Example

Imagine a trader, Paulette, has the 40 calls valued at 2.40 with the underlying stock price at $41. Consider this other relevant data for this trade:

- Call vega equals 0.05.
- Call delta equals 0.70 (or 70 per 100-share contract).
- Implied volatility on the 40 strike is 0.26.
- The trader's risk tolerance dictates that she should buy or sell up to $500 of vega (or, for this option, 100 contracts)

at any given volatility level before changing the volatility assumption.

- The trader's disseminated bid is 2.35, and the offer is 2.45 (0.10 wide).

Now imagine that an order to sell 1,000 calls at 2.35 enters the market. The trade consummation that follows sets up a chain of events. Paulette will pay 2.35 for 100 (we'll assume other market makers absorb the other 900 contracts). Because Paulette acquired 7,000 deltas (70 times 100 call contracts), she will immediately short 7,000 shares of the underlying stock at $41 to get delta neutral.

Paulette bought 100 options at a 0.05 vega (or $500 of position vega). Thus, her risk tolerance at this volatility level has been saturated. She would only be willing to buy more at a lower volatility level. In this case, she would lower the volatility assumption from 26 to 25. With a vega of 0.05, that would make the theoretical value of these calls 2.35 with the stock at $41. Again, that's 0.05 lower than 2.40, which it was with volatility at 26.

Consequently, Paulette's bid and ask will each fall by 5 cents. Her new market will be 2.30 bid, at 2.40 (with the stock price at $41). This market is centered around the new theoretical value of 2.35.

Trade P&L: Edge and Volatility

At this point, the trade has a measurable P&L associated with it. This trade has two influences on its profitability: edge and volatility. Let's examine the P&L, assuming the stock price remains unchanged at $41 and no other trades are made.

First, when the trade was initiated, the theoretical value was 2.40 with the stock at $41. The trader bought 100 contracts and hedged at $41. Therefore, the trader made a theoretical profit of $500—that's 5 cents per share of theoretical edge times 100 shares per contract times 100 contracts. However, Paulette then lowered her model volatility input by 1 point. That resulted in a loss of $500—that's 1 volatility point times 0.05 vega times 100 contracts. Therefore, her total theoretical P&L is zero, accounting for both edge and implied volatility.

Let's consider this trade from another perspective. With the stock at $41 and implied volatility at 26, the call was worth 2.40 and had a 0.05 vega. Thus, if Paulette paid 2.35 for the call, she "paid" a 25 volatility. Why? At a 25 implied volatility, the call is worth 2.35. She can use vega to calculate this easily in her head. Paulette paid 5 cents less than the theoretical value generated with a 26 volatility. She would lower volatility to make her new markets around a 25-volatility level. Therefore, because she paid a 25 volatility and is now running analytics at a 25 volatility, she has a P&L of zero.

In fact, traders often consider volatility as the commodity, noting the volatility level that they buy or sell (or bid or offer). In this context, consider that the original market was 25 bid at 27. With the stock at $41, the call bid price of 2.35 is a 25 volatility. The offer is 10 cents higher at 2.45. Based on vega, one can calculate that volatility to be 27—two volatility points higher.

Capturing Volatility Profits

This trade does not stand alone, nor does the stock price remain constant. Let's examine two scenarios that can play out and see how each would affect P&L.

In a perfect world, moments after buying (and hedging) these calls, a buy order for the same calls would come into the market, giving Paulette the opportunity to sell and take a 0.05 profit on a 100-lot trade. Imagine, for a moment, that this, indeed, occurs. An order to buy at least 100 of the 40 calls at 2.40 (the new offer) comes into the market, and the stock can still be traded at $41. Paulette would sell her 100 calls at 2.40 and buy back the 7,000 shares at $41.

The P&L is easy to calculate both in plain dollars and cents as well as in vega profits. Because Paulette paid 2.35 for 100 calls, sold 100 calls at 2.40, and scratched the stock (that is, bought and sold at $41 for a zero profit or loss), she made $500 (minus commissions)—that's the 5-cent options profit, times 100 shares per contract, times 100 contracts.

As for the P&L based on vega, it necessarily must come out to $500 as well. Paulette bought a 25 volatility (with the options at 2.35) and sold a 26 volatility (calls at 2.40). That's 1 volatility point times the 5-cent vega times 100 shares in the contract times 100 contracts—again, that's $500.

I can, literally, count on one hand the number of times such a scenario allowing for a quick scalp played out in my trading career. Usually, market makers must carry positions because they can't get out of the trade immediately—there usually doesn't just happen to be someone else in the world wanting to take the other side. Instead, they need to spread the near-substitutable options at other strikes or other months. This is where the latter calculation—vega-based P&L—really comes in handy.

These same calculations (dollars and cents, or vega P&L) can be observed more easily when risk tolerance is not saturated on a single trade, and thus the volatility input does not change. For example, initially, when Paulette had the option valued at 2.40 versus a $41 stock price, if she bought, say, 10 contracts at 0.35, she would not need to lower her volatility input. Therefore, she'd have simply made $50. In dollars and cents, that's simply 0.05 below the theoretical value of 2.40 times 10 contracts—or $50. In vega terms, that's 1 volatility point below the 26 volatility that Paulette is running times the 5-cent vega, times 10 contracts—again, $50.

Of course, Paulette would have hedged by selling 700 shares of stock at $41. Following this trade, Paulette would then hope to sell ideally on her same offer of $2.45 (27 volatility) and lock in $100 on the options and scratch the stock to eliminate the entire position. She'd likely settle for selling midmarket at $2.40 (her theoretical value run at the 26 volatility level). She'd then scratch the stock and lock in a $50 profit while eliminating the position risk.

Vega-Based P&L on a Spread

Consider the original trade: one hundred 40-strike calls are bought at the 25 volatility level, hedged with 7,000 shares of stock at $41; assume the trader has lowered the volatility assumption to 25. Now imagine a market order to buy the *45 calls* comes into the market. Consider the following trade data assumptions for the 45 calls:

- The stock is at $41.
- There is no vertical skew (the implied volatility on the 45 strike is 25).
- The 45-call theoretical value equals 0.51.
- The 45-call delta equals 0.20 (or, 20 per 100-share contract).

- The 45-call vega equals 0.04.
- The trader disseminates a 0.10-wide market; the bid is 0.45, and the offer is 0.55.
- The trader's offer is equal to the National Best Bid and Offer (NBBO).

In this example, Paulette sells one hundred 45 calls at 0.55 and immediately hedges by buying 2,000 shares of stock at $41. This is a very important trade, in relation to the first trade, the 40 calls. First, by selling the 45 calls, Paulette has "locked in" a theoretical edge in terms of volatility. At a 25 volatility, the calls are valued at 0.51, but Paulette has sold them at 0.55. Because the call is 0.04 higher than theoretical value, and vega is 0.04, she has sold a 26 volatility.

Paulette has effectively legged into a debit call spread (delta neutral) for 1 volatility point of edge while reducing risk. The vega risk has been cut down to a fraction of the risk of either individual leg of the spread. The 40 calls contribute to being long $500 of position vega; the 45 calls give short $400 of position vega. Thus, the net position is long only $100 of vega. If Paulette raises or lowers her volatility assumption, it will only slightly affect her theoretical P&L—that is, her vega profits or losses.

Paulette would simply adjust the volatility input to match that which is trading in the market as a result of order flow beyond her control. The ultimate end game is to eventually leg back out of the trade for fair value or, ideally, for more edge. These, in essence, are the mechanics of market-maker trading.

To make the example realistic, we would eliminate the assumption that there is no vertical volatility skew. In fact, some skew would be likely to exist. But so long as market makers buy options below the skewed theoretical value and sell them above that value while opening and subsequently closing positions, they are gaining theoretical edge and locking in real profits. Now, let's also eliminate the assumption that the stock price has remained constant.

How Volatility Normalizes Underlying Price Movement
Let's return, once again, to the initial 40-call trade. Observe the following trade data:

- One hundred 40 calls bought at 2.35 (25 volatility) delta neutral by shorting 7,000 shares at $41.
- The theoretical value of the 40 calls is 2.40, with values run at 26 volatility.
- Market implied volatility remains constant.
- *The trader keeps volatility assumption constant, still running theoretical values at 26* following the trade.
- The call vega equals 0.05.
- The call delta with the stock at $41 equals 0.70 (or, 70 per 100-share contract).
- The trader's market is always 0.10 wide.

Consider what would happen if the underlying stock were to fall, say, 50 cents to $40.50 on the initial trade date and Paulette was able to sell the calls on her offer. She might make money, but there would be a few more iterations in the calculation. First, we must start with projecting the theoretical value for the calls with the underlying stock at $40.50.

The arithmetic for the new value is rather straightforward. The value is currently 2.40. The formula for calculating an option value is delta times the change in the underlying asset—in this case, 0.70 delta times (negative) 50 cents equals a decline of 35 cents in call value. With the stock at $40.50, the 40-strike call's theoretical value would be 2.05 (2.40 minus 0.35).

Paulette's market would be 2.00 bid at 2.10 (again, 0.10 wide). If, indeed, an order to buy on the offer entered the market and she sold 100 contracts, she'd sell them at 2.10.

So far, it appears as if Paulette has lost money: she bought the calls at 2.35 and sold at 2.10. However, consider the hedge. She shorted 7,000 shares at $41 and would then buy them back at $40.50. So we have the following pair of trades:

Bought 100 calls at 2.35; sold 100 calls at 2.10	Lost: $2,500
Shorted 7,000 shares at $41; bought 7,000 shares at $40.50	Made: $3,500
Trade P&L	Made: $1,000

The profitability, in this case, is easy to decipher. Paulette bought 100 calls 0.05 below theoretical value for $500 of theoretical edge. She closed the trade by selling the 100 calls 0.05 over the theoretical value for $500 of edge. Upon closing the position, she eliminated future risk and locked in $1,000 of *actual* profits. When open positions are closed, *theoretical* edge becomes *actual* P&L.

In vega terms, Paulette bought 100 calls at a 25 volatility and sold them at a 27 volatility. The P&L is calculated as 2 volatility points profit times 5-cent vega, times 100 contracts equals a $1,000 profit. This is why vega is so useful and important in calculating P&L. In this calculation, the option price and the stock price don't factor in. It is purely a volatility calculation: At what volatility level did she buy it? And, at what volatility level did she sell it?

A Note on Gamma and Theta

In fact, the profit on this trade could be greater or less than the $1,000 shown. It could be more, particularly if the movement in the underlying were bigger—say, $2, $3, or even $5. Given a movement in the underlying stock, deltas change as a result of gamma. Because long options have positive gamma, the deltas would change in favor of the trader. As the stock falls, gamma creates negative deltas. As the stock rises, gamma creates positive deltas. Traders capture profits on these changing deltas by hedging with more stock as the market rises or buying stock back at a profit when the market falls to get back to being delta neutral, potentially scalping if the stock oscillates. But the profit could be less as well. If time passes, theta factors into P&L. The effect of these influences (gamma and theta) can be considered the effect of realized volatility.

INSIDER STRATEGIES FROM THE TRADING FLOOR

Much of this chapter has been in the context of the professional market-making trader. Nonprofessionals aspiring to success must understand these mechanics to understand the motivations of liquidity providers and thus the options market in general. But nonprofessionals can also trade some strategies formerly reserved for only the pros. One such insider strategy that has been gaining popularity since the advent of retail portfolio margining is gamma scalping. Gamma scalping, a topic that is discussed at length in the next chapter, is a sort of crossover strategy for trading straddles, synthetic straddles, and perhaps more complex derivatives of the straddle.

14

VOLATILITY
AND STRADDLES
The Market-Maker Trade

I was teaching a class one day at the Chicago Board Options Exchange, and between sessions I struck up a conversation with one of the students. He explained that he was enjoying the class, but what he really wanted to do was to "learn gamma scalping—like what market makers do." I asked him why he wanted to learn that particular trading technique. He replied, "Because that's where the money is."

Having spent most of my professional career as a gamma scalper, I can attest that it is possible for someone to make money with this method—perhaps a lot of money. But it is not necessarily better than any other style of trading. It serves a very unique purpose. In fact, some strategies should *only* be traded using the gamma-scalping technique.

THE SUCKER BET

Let's examine the long straddle. A long straddle consists of a long call and a long put sharing the same strike, with the same expiration month, and on the same underlying asset. But empirically, I believe the straddle has, possibly, the poorest results of all traded strategies among retail traders. Curiously, professional traders trade them all the time and can do well. So why do so many retail traders fail with this simple strategy? *Because they don't do it right*.

Many traders read a basic options book, see an at-expiration P&L diagram of a straddle, and think trading straddles is easy. They make the mistake of trading straddles as "breakeven-point strategies." Novice traders buy a straddle and hope that the underlying asset moves enough to break the barrier of the upper or lower breakeven price on the at-expiration P&L diagram. This, under most circumstances, is a *sucker bet*.

The straddle is a volatility play, which must capitalize on volatility pricing and natural permutations of volatility in the underlying asset. Looking for a big move in either direction is a less likely realized volatility permutation than back-and-forth oscillation of smaller price action. Look at a chart of any stock, bond, commodity or other tradable asset and notice that even in trends, there are up days and down days—a natural oscillation. These are the moves that straddles are designed to capture. Breakeven-point straddle trades miss the peaks and troughs. To trade a straddle effectively generally requires gamma scalping.

GAMMA SCALPING

Gamma scalping is a technique in which a trader holds an overall long-option position and trades it in a delta-neutral fashion. But because long-option positions have (positive) gamma, deltas change when the underlying asset price changes. When the deltas change, traders trade the underlying asset to recalibrate their positions to return to being delta neutral.

Because the long straddle's gamma is positive, deltas always change in favor of the trader, getting longer when the underlying asset rallies and shorter when the underlying asset falls. To hedge acquired deltas, traders must sell stock when the underlying stock rises and buy stock when the underlying stock falls. Hence, the term "gamma scalping." In an oscillating market, this process results in profitable scalping transactions in the underlying asset.

For example, a trader, Eileen, buys fifty 80-strike straddles delta neutral (with the underlying stock at $79.50). Both the call and the put have a 0.06 gamma. Therefore, the gamma of the position is 6, or 600, in terms of position deltas per contract. (That's 0.06 gamma times 100 shares per contact times 100 total options [50 calls and 50 puts].)

Here's how gamma scalping works. Imagine the underlying stock rises $1 to $80.50. Because of gamma, the straddle position will grow to be long 600 deltas (that's 600 gammas times a $1 move). Eileen would short 600 shares of stock at $80.50 to return to being delta neutral (i.e., zero delta).

Now imagine the underlying stock falls down $1, back to $79.50. Gamma will result in the straddle plus the short position of 600 shares now being short 600 deltas. Thus, Eileen would buy back her 600 shares at $79.50 to get flat deltas again. Recall that the straddle without the stock has a zero delta at $79.50. With the 600 short shares, she'd be short 600 deltas with the stock at $79.50. If she buys back the 600 shares at $79.50 to close out the short position, she's back to being flat deltas.

In this example, the rise and fall of the underlying stock resulted in Eileen profitably scalping stock (shorting 600 at $80.50, then buying 600 at $79.50) for the goal of remaining delta neutral. But there's more to this trade. Specifically, there is negative theta—and all the decision making that goes along with it. In short, traders must determine whether the amount of theta given up each passing day is acceptable per the expected daily P&L from scalping.

For example, at first glance, if Eileen thought that she could scalp an average of $600 every day, she'd be content with a straddle position that had a total theta position of less than $600 a day. But she'd have to adjust for weekends. She could only scalp Monday through Friday—five days a week. Theta is based on a seven-day weekly calendar. Hence, she would accept anything less than a $429 daily theta ($600 expected daily scalp, times 5 days of scalping, divided by 7 days in the theta week).

Though this logic appears very straightforward, it can get a little more complex. Implied volatility and vega necessarily come into play. One needs to examine the theta of the trade from the perspective of volatility.

How Volatility Affects Theta

For the next examples, we will assume that Eileen has a crystal ball and can see the future. She knows with certainty that every day the stock will rise exactly $1 and then fall exactly $1.

Example: 20 Volatility

Imagine that Eileen's 50-lot straddle costs her 5.45 (2.55 for the calls, 2.90 for the puts) with the following trade parameters:

- Volatility is 20.
- There are 67 days until expiration.
- The position theta is $200 (0.02 for both the call and the put per contract, times 100 total contracts).
- The total position gamma is 600.

Given the crystal-ball assumption and the trade parameters above, would Eileen want to buy this straddle? Certainly. She knows that each week she must pay $1,400 in theta ($200 times 7 calendar days), but she makes $3,000 a week ($600 times 5 trading days).

Example: 40 Volatility

But what if she had to pay more for the straddle? Would she still buy it? If volatility instead were at 40, the call would be 5.25 and the put would be 5.60, making the straddle worth 10.85. But there would still be 67 days until expiration. At expiration, time premium will be zero. That means, the higher-priced straddle must decay at a faster rate than it would if the straddle was priced lower at, say, a 20 volatility. *It must, therefore, have a higher theta.* And it does. The theta is about 0.04 for the call and also for the put. The total position theta is, therefore, $400 a day (0.04 times 100 contracts).

But theta is not the only greek affected by the higher volatility input. So is gamma. Gamma gets smaller as volatility rises (all else held constant). With volatility at 40, the gamma of the 40-volatility straddle is 0.03 per option, or 300 position deltas (for the 100 total options). That means, if—per the crystal-ball assumption—the stock rises $1 and falls $1, Eileen would short 300 shares and buy back the 300 shares for a scalp of only $300.

So for a week, Eileen would pay $2,800 ($400 times 7) in theta and scalp for $1,500 ($300 times 5). The higher volatility is prohibitive for this trade. With the same price movement, she can't profit given the cost of the straddle.

Gamma and Theta's Alter Egos: Realized and Implied Volatility

The situational assumption in this scenario is that Eileen knows with clairvoyance that the stock will rise and fall exactly $1 each day. Generally speaking, this is not a realistic assumption (though, at one time, I did trade in the same pit with a guy who told me, in all seriousness, that he traded based on psychically knowing what would happen and could also bend spoons with his mind, to boot). However, Eileen can forecast expected realized volatility.

Realized volatility is price movement. Gamma scalps capture profits as a result of realized volatility in the underlying asset. The greater the realized volatility, the more scalping a trader can do given the same amount of gamma. To measure how much revenue gamma scalping is likely to bring in, traders must assess realized volatility.

But as in any other business, traders must consider not just the expected revenue but also the expenses. For example, the implied volatility level at which the straddle can be purchased ultimately determines the theta expense. The comparison of expected revenues to expenses is as simple as comparing current implied volatility to expected realized volatility.

Implied and realized volatility are stated in the same units: annualized standard deviation. This makes for a straightforward analysis. Traders must aspire to "buy" an implied volatility that is lower than what they forecast future realized volatility to be. This is buying value.

Buying value in volatility doesn't entirely guarantee success. But it offers a statistical likelihood of success. For one, some skill on behalf of the trader is necessary to not underscalp and miss opportunities; or overscalp and capture moves that are too small. But, also, volatility can manifest itself in different ways.

There are a seemingly infinite number of permutations that can result in a unique realized volatility number. Volatility is made up of the magnitude of asset-price movements over a fixed period of time. There can be more up days than down days, more down days than up days, an equal number of up and down days, some bigger movement days than others, and so on. But one thing is certain: a permutation leading to a certain volatility in which most price action is entirely in one direction is less likely than a more random oscillation.

That brings us to the original point: trading straddles as breakeven-point strategies is a sucker bet. While it is not uncommon for some stocks to trend strongly or have sharp breakouts in either direction, it is more likely that there are pullbacks, petering-out trends, and other scenarios that lead to prices being centered more around the mean than away from it. This is the premise of every commonly used option-pricing model: a lognormally distributed probability curve.

This case is further made when using delta as an estimation for the likelihood of an option expiring in-the-money. Imagine the March 50 straddle can be bought for 5. In this case, the at-expiration breakevens would be $45 to the downside and $55 to the upside. Incidentally, the 45-strike put coincides with the downside breakeven. The delta of the 45 put in this example is 0.17. The 55 call strike happens to coincide with the upside breakeven. The 55 call's delta is 0.22.

The respective deltas imply the estimation that if the straddle is held until expiration without gamma scalping, there is a 17 percent chance of it being profitable to the downside (i.e., a 17 percent chance of the 45 put being in-the-money) and a 22 percent chance of it being profitable to the upside (of the call being in-the-money). And, of course, only one scenario (up *or* down) can come to fruition. Thus, the chances of this straddle—traded as a breakeven-point trade—being a winner at expiration, though not impossible, is statistically unlikely.

THE STRATEGY OF THE PROS

Gamma scalping is an active strategy that requires near constant monitoring. For that reason, it is for professionals or stay-at-home traders who are serious about trading. Furthermore, it requires comparatively big positions to make a big enough profit. Case in point, the example used throughout this chapter centered around a 50-lot straddle in which each day a mere few hundred dollars was likely to be made or lost. Even P&L resulting from implied volatility fluctuations, as discussed in the last chapter, is likely to be small on a per-option basis, compared to more retail-oriented strategies. Therefore, gamma scalpers must have the liberal margins of either a professional trader like a market maker or retail portfolio margining.

Trading Straddles Professionally

I have personally traded lots of straddles in my years as a professional trader. In fact, one could say that that is all I traded. Because as a market maker everything was (for the most part) done delta neutral, one could make the case that any trade I made was quickly converted to a synthetic straddle or a synthetic straddle spread.

For example, recall that synthetically

$$\text{Long Call} + \text{Short Stock} = \text{Long Put}$$

Imagine a trader buys 100 at-the-money calls and sells 5,000 shares as a hedge to get delta neutral. Effectively, the trader has bought 50 straddles. How? We can separate out this trade into calls and synthetic puts:

$$50 \text{ Long Calls} + (50 \text{ Long Calls} + \text{Short 5,000 Shares})$$

where 50 Long Calls + Short 5,000 Shares = 50 Synthetic Long Puts

Delta neutral, this trade has no directional exposure until gamma creates deltas. With no immediate directional risk, this trade has only volatility risk. It has positive gamma, negative theta, and positive vega. It's all volatility risk: it's all straddle.

AIT Gamma Trade

In my first few years as a market maker, one of the option classes I traded in my pit was Ameritech (AIT)—which was gobbled up by SBC Communications, which became AT&T Inc. (T). (Incidentally, the symbol AIT now belongs to a different company.) Ameritech didn't really trend much during that time. It just kind of traded sideways for a couple of years. It was a nice one for retail traders who like to sell credit spreads, iron condors, and the like. This ended up being very good for me.

Income traders sold options to us market makers. I was usually overall long gamma in this stock for a couple of years. But despite the fact that it was a fairly sideways stock, it had some volatility. It would rise and/or fall a dollar or so almost every day. I made money on this stock just about every day scalping gamma. By the end of the year, it was usually one of my biggest winners.

The Long and the Short of It

In AIT, or any long gamma trade I made, I wasn't long every strike all the time. Of course, there were some option buyers to whom I sold options, and some spread traders. I was just *net* long gamma (options). But I was short some strikes too. When the stock moved from a long strike to a short strike, the overall position could take on the characteristics of a short straddle. If the gamma is negative and theta positive and the position is delta neutral, that is synthetically what exists—a short straddle. When the underlying asset is nearest a long strike, the overall position can act like a long straddle; when the underlying asset is nearest a short strike, the position can act like a short straddle.

SHORT GAMMA MANAGEMENT

Short straddles are basically the opposite of long straddles (short a call and a put in the same expiration month, same strike, on the same underlying asset). But the management of short-gamma positions is slightly different from their long-gamma counterparts.

Whenever a long gamma scalper makes a hedge trade, he or she is always "right." Every long-gamma hedge locks in a realized volatility profit. But when a trader hedges negative gamma, he or she is always "wrong." Short-gamma hedges always lock in a loss.

For example, imagine a trader is short 40 of the September 60 straddles and the position is exactly delta neutral and is negative 700 position gammas. Now imagine that the underlying stock rises $2. Because of gamma, the trader would be short 1,400 deltas. Although the position started delta neutral, as the underlying stock rose, it gained a short directional bias with each tick higher in the underlying stock.

The trade definitely lost money at an increasing rate as the underlying stock rose. When the underlying stock was 50 cents higher, the position was short 350 deltas (meaning it would lose money in a rising market as if it were short 350 shares). Another 50 cents higher, the position would be short 700 deltas and would lose as the stock rose as if it were short 700 shares. Up another 50 cents, the position would be short 1,050 deltas, and would lose like a position short 1,050 shares as the stock rises. And so on.

If the straddle trader in this example thinks the rise in share price will continue higher, he or she will need to buy the underlying stock to cover the negative delta (locking in a loss), to get back to delta neutral. The risk, of course, is that the trader buys shares to cover and the stock retraces, falling back down, leading to a negative scalp on the stock-purchase hedge. Again, negative gamma hedges are always wrong. Traders sometimes must hedge to stem further losses, but they must be very selective as to when to do so.

Techniques for Negative Gamma Hedging

There are many techniques that professional traders use to cover deltas acquired from negative gamma. These are several common techniques from which to choose:

Standard deviation About two-thirds of all price movements are expected to fall within up one standard deviation and down one standard deviation. Cover when the underlying permeates the up or down daily standard deviation based on implied volatility.

Support and resistance When the underlying asset breaks through support or resistance on a price chart of the underlying, it could indicate a breakout in that direction. Cover when either is violated.

Dollars lost All traders have a pain threshold. Once you lose a certain amount of money, cover.

Percentage move Once the underlying moves a certain percentage, cover.

Acquired deltas Delta risk can be the biggest risk in option trading. Once gamma leads to the position being long or short a certain number of deltas, get back to neutral.

Hedge half Can't decide when to hedge? Cover half of the deltas. Doing so stems further losses, but the trader doesn't lose as much if the underlying asset retraces.

Adjusting Retail Income Trades

When considering negative-gamma hedging from the perspective of covering acquired deltas with the underlying asset, it is easy to understand how losses occur and how they are locked in. But the same thing happens with negative-gamma .retail income trades, such as iron condors, butterflies, and others. Often these trades start out delta neutral and then the underlying asset moves, leading to adverse deltas. By definition, that means the trade would be losing money.

Traders are generally more concerned about the "end game" with these strategies, focusing more on theta and the at-expiration breakevens than negative gamma. Many retail traders have a great lust for adjusting income trades when the underlying asset moves too far. But what many traders don't realize is that every time they adjust the trade (neutralizing the delta), they too are locking in a loss. Novice income traders are easily tricked, drawn by the siren song of fashionable adjusting. Because adjusting with options is not as uni-dimensional as adjusting with the underlying asset, it is easy to get fooled into thinking that a loss is not being locked in—*but it is*.

The difference is that hedging with options incurs a position in the other greeks, aside from delta (contrary to hedging with the delta-only underlying asset). So adjustments may provide additional theta, additional "wiggle room" by making the breakeven(s) farther away from the money, or additional time for the trade to reap the benefits of time decay. Positions in these option-centric pricing influences may overcome the loss locked in by covering deltas. In fact, that is what good adjustments are meant to do. Retail income traders often *must* make adjustments to repair positions gone awry. But they need to make them sparingly.

15

ARBITRAGE AND NICHE TRADING
How Small Profits Add Up to Big Money

It is human nature to be risk averse. Risk takers such as cliff divers, daredevils, and other adventurers are drawn to risk for the thrill of what they know might harm them. They go against that which is inherent in the pursuit of excitement. As children, we hear stories of great adventurers who face risk after risk in their journeys. But as adults, we realize the tales we read as children are of finite timelines in an adventurer's life. In reality, if the risk-taking hero keeps taking his chances, at some point he's going to bite the dust.

Experienced veteran traders know this. They've traded a lot; they've seen it all. They know what fate ultimately awaits the risk taker. Though retail traders can get lucky in perpetuity if they are only making a few trades a month, professional traders who make a hundred trades a day or more can't press their luck forever.

In my trading career, I've seen trades play out in ways that I couldn't have imagined possible. Four and five standard deviation events played out more than they should have—*leptokurtosis, for sure*. I've had a good number of disasters and a good number of windfalls. For example, the market drop following September 11, 2001, resulted in my losing $320,000 from my account all hitting at once the moment the market opened days later. I've also occasionally walked onto the floor in the morning to see a stock up or down on a surprise gap, starting the day with a windfall profit. In time, I learned to try to avoid both pleasant and unpleasant surprises in favor of a surer thing. That is what all traders who enjoy longevity in their careers do.

THEORETICAL PRICING

The concept of theoretical pricing focuses on making trades more of a sure thing. Ultimately, all a trader knows about the value of any option is *if this is worth this, then that must be worth that*. And so it goes that in tight, liquid markets, market makers buy a penny or two below their theoretical values and sell a penny or two above them. As long as trades are delta hedged, the greatest part of their risk is abated in favor of the less uncertain risks. Traders lean on one option or the underlying asset to trade another option.

THE PICK-OFF, OR THE NEEDLE IN THE HAYSTACK

In trading there is always fear of getting picked off—that is, being taken advantage of by another, predatory trader. Ask a typical retail trader about market makers and you're likely to get an earful about how market makers are always picking retail traders off. Ask a market maker about retail traders and, likewise, you'll get a conspiracy theory about retail traders picking off the market makers. The fact is that nowadays there is very little picking off going on—finding a bona fide pick-off is like finding a needle in a haystack.

But in the name of arbitrage, there are some professional traders who make a living keeping the market in check looking for pricing discrepancies to exploit—they look for those proverbial needles. Undoubtedly, traders get picked off only when they allow it to happen. Pick-offs are about arbitrage. Clever traders trading lower-risk niches, arbitrage, or near-arbitrage trades should identify these opportunities on their own. The goal is to find arbitrage opportunities before they find you.

THE ART OF THE LEAN

There are lots of niches exploited by professional traders and savvy stay-at-home traders alike. All trading niches revolve around leans pitting one option value against another. Essentially, when traders exploit niches and arbitrage opportunities, they are trading an iterative asset class that is only somewhat related to the original asset class. The asset traded is typically the differential value between the legs of the trade.

Pairs Trading

A simple example, and a rather common niche, is the pairs trade. As the name implies, a pairs trade involves trading a pair of assets. Pairs trading can be done with two stocks, two ETFs, two indexes, two futures, or two options (on different, but usually related, option classes).

For example, a trader may buy shares in the Standard & Poor's Depositary Receipts (SPY) and short shares in the iShares Russell 2000 Index Fund (IWM). The rationale for such a trade in this example would be that SPY will outperform IWM. These ETFs are similar with much overlap, yet they are different. They will likely move somewhat in sync with one another. But the trade is the spread. Both may rise, both may fall, but it is the spread widening or tightening that makes or loses money. Typically, with equities or ETFs, traders buy and sell the same dollar value of shares, pitting percentage moves against each other as opposed to nominal moves.

When options are the components of a pairs trade, the asset being traded is typically the volatility differential. Traders might buy calls in McDonald's Corp. (MCD) and sell calls in Yum! Brands, Inc. (YUM). When the intent is to exploit the differential of the volatility spread widening or tightening, each option leg will likely be done delta neutral. In this example, the trader would be positioning for MCD volatility to outperform YUM volatility. Again, both options' volatility may rise; both may fall. The trade is the volatility differential.

Both the directional outperformance (shares) trade—in this case, the ETFs—and the volatility outperformance (options) trade—MCD vs. YUM—are iteratively removed from the performance of the underlying ETF or corporation. The spread differential positioning is a very different trade from a simple directional trade or a volatility trade. It is an iterative step *farther*. The pairs trade is likely to be less risky than a conventional direction or volatility trade, particularly when assets are highly correlated. It is also likely to have less potential reward. Thus, trade size is usually bigger for these types of trades, requiring traders to be well capitalized.

Volatility Trading

Volatility is in and of itself a lean trade, as has been discussed throughout much of this book. When a trader hedges to get delta neutral, he or she may make money on the option portion of the position and lose on the underlying portion, or vice versa. The trader cares little about which leg is a winner or a loser. The trader cares only about the incremental delta creation (resulting from gamma), incremental time decay (of theta), and incremental changes in volatility (vega). Small changes in these option-centric pricing influences are being traded. Success of a delta-neutral volatility trade is conceptually far removed from the profitability of the corporation on which the options are listed.

Skew Trading

One step further in complexity than straight volatility trading is skew trading. As discussed, there typically exists vertical volatility skew in most optionable asset classes. In equity options (along with ETFs and indexes), typically the lower the strike, the higher the volatility. The "fear" is to the downside. This is often represented in vertical skew.

Skew is well defined in a given option class. It is mathematically stated as up slopes (for option strikes higher-than-the-money) and down slopes (for lower-than-the-money option strikes). For equity options, down slopes are typically steeper than up slopes. The values on the slopes are sometimes calculated linearly and sometimes exponentially—there is some debate within the industry. But, logically, volatilities must be in some sort of line.

It is easy to see how each successive lower put strike may be of more value to a trader—cheaper insurance, for one; also greater fear of bigger declines. Here's an example of volatility skew:

50 strike	40 volatility
45 strike	42 volatility
40 strike	44 volatility
35 strike	46 volatility

This scenario shows a logical, linear down slope with each lower strike getting successively higher (in this case, by 2 volatility points per \$5 strike increment).

It would be very illogical for strikes to be nonlinear. For example,

50 strike	40 volatility
45 strike	42 volatility
40 strike	38 volatility
35 strike	46 volatility

Certainly, the 40 strike would not have less utility than its flanking neighbors, the 45 and 35 strikes; therefore, its volatility should not be lower than both. This scenario would indicate a discrepancy leading to an arbitrage-like opportunity. A rational arbitrageur would sell the 35-40-45 butterfly, by selling one 35 call, buying two 40 calls, and selling one 45 call and then hedging the net delta.

There are plenty of traders watching the skew in every single optionable asset. They keep volatility skews in line and rational. Market makers run their theoretical values with skewed volatilities, buying cheap volatility and selling expensive volatility relative to the skewed theoreticals. Proprietary traders who trade volatility also watch skews.

There are a few different opportunities that arise in skew trading. Sometimes skews get slightly out of line, leading to a kink, or a bump, in the slope. Sometimes skews adjust, getting higher or lower; for example, if traders are particularly worried about downside risk in a particular stock, the down slope may readjust, making lower strikes worth even more than usual relative to higher strikes. Skew traders here would capitalize on the opportunity by buying put spreads (buying the higher-strike put, and selling the lower-strike put) delta neutral.

But in skew trading, like most niches, there is not usually a great deal of risk or reward per contract in skew trading (except in extreme circumstances). Thus, mostly only well-capitalized professional traders can make this trade work by doing big enough trades.

DISPERSION MODELS AND MORE

Over the past few years, a particular evolution of arbitrage has gained popularity: the dispersion model. Dispersion-model trading is a sophisticated type of volatility spreading similar to pairs trading but with lots more options comprising a master spread. The general philosophy is that the implied volatilities of options listed on a basket (an ETF or an index) are mathematically related to the implied volatilities of the component option classes. Thus, when volatilities get out of line, a mathematical arbitrage-like opportunity exists.

This general concept of model trading has been around for a while. But we've seen more and more of it lately. In the early 2000s, securities options exchanges became home to many groups of traders trading models. Over the past couple of years, even the commodity exchanges have seen a sharp uptick in the number of model trading groups.

Model trading is not for everyone. It requires a big operation and lots of money. In general, traders need to trade just about every class that can be traded. That is easy enough in the grain complex, where groups trade corn volatility against soybean volatility against wheat volatility. That requires only a handful of traders in each of those pits, a crack computer staff, deep pockets, and, of course, the brains behind it all to dream up the math for the model.

On securities exchanges in which equities, ETFs, and indexes are traded, these groups may consist of 50 or more traders on a single exchange. Traders need to be actively engaged in trading all liquid option classes in order to maximize exploitation of volatility dispar-ities across the market. Further, because fungible securities options are traded on multiple exchanges that may have small volatility dis-crepancies, groups need to populate multiple exchanges.

In model trading, the margins are very thin. I've seen traders in some of these groups make markets a penny wide. To make these miniscule margins worthwhile and to cover overhead costs, traders need to trade big—and by that, I mean *really big*. It is not uncommon for some of these groups to be among the biggest market makers in a particular option class. Sometimes these traders are 1,000 up or more (that is, on both the bid and the offer), a penny or two wide.

These traders provide two very important functions in the options market: they provide lots of liquidity and contribute to volatility-pricing efficiency. They keep prices in line with where they "should be" by buying volatility when it gets too cheap and selling it when it gets too expensive (even by a penny or two), rela-tive to comparable option classes.

NICHES, ARBITRAGE, AND THE RETAIL TRADER

Many of the techniques discussed in this chapter are for well-capi-talized traders or trading firms that can survive on paper-thin mar-gins because of the size they trade. But even though these strategies are not conducive to nonarbitrageurs, clever stay-at-home traders can borrow some of these techniques and adapt them to their own trading styles. Particularly, the concept of dispersion model trading can be adapted easily and worked into even a basic retail portfolio. With good portfolio management, both professional and retail traders can simplify this technique to truncate risk and gain edge.

16

MONITORING OPTIONS PORTFOLIO RISK

The fictional character Harry Callahan (a.k.a. Dirty Harry) once said, "A man's got to know his limitations." When it comes to trading, no truer words were ever spoken.

GETTING YOUR PIECE OF THE PIE WITHOUT LOSING YOUR LUNCH

After I passed the CBOE's membership exam to become a member of the exchange, the next step was to decide in which pit I was going to trade. I had a rather simple approach. I looked up the volume data for the past few months in some of the pits I was thinking about, counted the number of traders in each of those pits, and divided volume by the number of traders.

The thought was that, once in the pit, I would compete fiercely for my *share*—my piece of the pie—and try to get even more. As a well-capitalized trader, I wanted to trade as much as I could. I wasn't down on the exchange floor to "make a nice living" or "beat the S&P 500." I was there to be a *big* trader; to take all the money I could out of the pit I was in. And why wouldn't I? I had the capital behind me. Just as competing corporations battle to be the industry leader—the biggest and the best—likewise, I was in it to win it. When an order came into the pit, I wanted the biggest piece of it I could get. But, as they say, "Be careful what you wish for."

Unmanageably big positions can easily add up from making trade after trade. And, undoubtedly, sometimes a single trade can be too big to handle. Traders must show some restraint. Every once in a while, a broker would come into the pit and say, "Sold at such-and-such price." I'd say, "I'll buy 'em. How many do you have?" and he'd just smile. That's always when I knew I'd better be careful.

That sick feeling traders get from having too big of a loss resulting from too big of a position carried for too long? One pit trader in the pit called it "reaching the stomach-turning point." It's the point at which you just can't handle it any more and have to *puke out of the trade* (closing it down and locking in a loss to get out). Puking out of a trade is an evil fate that, surely, every market maker has had to do from time to time. The remedy is usually a little preventative medicine, or more precisely, a little self-restraint. Again, *a man's got to know his limitations*.

RISK LIMITS AND MANAGING POSITIONS

All traders, whether market makers, prop traders, or small-potatoes stay-at-homes, must set risk limits. Options are instruments of leverage, and some strategies have unlimited loss potential. Traders must truncate risk to avoid huge losses when very unlikely events occur.

Nowadays, students of trading and I spend a lot of time talking about options portfolio management. I have some strong opinions and give students regimented rules to follow. But I didn't invent the idea of portfolio risk limits. It is what any halfway decent market maker learns to do from day one. I simply bring the professional traders' techniques to the masses.

As a market maker, I had a risk manager who would expect me to trade within certain limits. If I went beyond my limits, I needed to hedge, close part of the trade, or find some other creative way to get back within my limits. Again, risk limits must be set and followed by all traders, professional or otherwise. Risk limits are not subjective: *they are law.*

CASH AND CASH RESERVES

Managing cash is also an important part of managing an options portfolio. All options portfolios consist of capital applied to option or stock positions and some amount of cash. The capital applied to options is called "margin." In the options nomenclature, margin is the amount of capital your broker requires you to put up to carry an option position. Margin is somewhat a measure of both leverage and protection.

Part of the value of an options portfolio should always be cash. Cash serves many purposes in an options account. First, cash is the resource that gets allocated to option positions; it provides the potential to seize opportunities. Traders must keep a reserve of cash for initiating new trades and to adjust positions in inventory.

Second, cash is an asset in and of itself. When the market is not conducive to trading or when a trader simply can't find a good trade, cash is a conservative asset in which to invest.

Because cash is an asset within a portfolio, trading results include the cash portion of the portfolio. When end-of-month (EOM) or end-of-year (EOY) results are stated in percentage terms, they're stated on the whole portfolio—including cash. For example, imagine a trader has a $100,000 account. The trader leaves $50,000 in cash and buys $50,000 worth of options. If the options portion of the account doubles in value, gaining $50,000, the portfolio will be worth $150,000 ($50,000 in cash; $100,000 in options). Thus, the trader has made 50 percent on the portfolio—*not* 100 percent.

All traders have a finite amount of cash. They must allocate it effectively. The consequences of not having enough cash deployed in options positions are low EOY results and missed opportunities.

Deploying too much cash results in being overleveraged and not having enough cash reserves for initiating trades and adjusting.

So, how much is the right amount to hold in cash reserves? The answer to this question is situational and personal. It is contingent upon the market and the trader's risk tolerance. Sometimes the market offers greater opportunity and thus demands that more capital be applied. Traders who trade highly leveraged positions may keep more in cash than traders with less leveraged positions to counterweight speculative trades. Aggressive traders with speculative but less directionally leveraged positions, however, may deploy more cash than do others.

As a general rule of thumb, a reasonable cash reserves amount should be between 15 and 30 percent of a total option-trading portfolio that is fully exploited. This range should allow enough working capital to adjust and capture opportunities and also to be diversified somewhat in a safe-haven asset. Less-experienced traders should hold much more in cash and trade smaller positions than veteran traders do.

OBSERVING PORTFOLIO RISK

Portfolio risk can be observed in the context of absolute risk or incremental risk. Absolute risk (or reward) is, as the name implies, *absolute* under any circumstance. Such risk includes very large movements in the underlying stock or market or the evaporation of all time premium. Thus, absolute risk is indicated by an at-expiration P&L diagram. Incremental risk is the risk of incremental changes in any of the pricing influences on options' value. Incremental risk is usually more useful because most experienced option traders close positions before expiration. This risk is measured by the greeks. Both absolute and incremental risk must be monitored and limited.

POSITION P&L DIAGRAMS

Option risk management is fractal. Each individual option has risk and must be monitored. And, as each option spread is made up of individual options, it too has risk and must be watched carefully.

Likewise, each option class may be made up of more than one spread and thus must be paid close attention to as a unit of risk. And each portfolio, made up of multiple option classes, has risk and must be monitored. Indeed, an entire options portfolio can be thought of as a single trade.

Many options user interfaces create P&L diagrams for an entire options portfolio. A P&L diagram is a great tool for monitoring systematic risk. It is simple and easy to understand (though it requires a computer to do the calculations and graphing). It is valuable, because it visually represents the portfolio as a single (possibly massive) position. But it is somewhat limited. For one, a P&L diagram doesn't show incremental risk such as theta and vega. So traders must set risk thresholds and sliding risk limits.

RISK THRESHOLDS

Risk thresholds are maximum boundaries established for various risk metrics. Specifically, traders set maximum values for position greeks and total portfolio greeks—again, looking at risk management fractally.

Position Risk Thresholds

Setting position risk thresholds is a lot like budgeting. The first step is to know how much you have available. In this context, that means traders must know their risk tolerance per position. For example: *How many deltas do I have to spend on each trade? How many vegas can I afford to put on a single position?*

On the exchange, traders strive to spread to keep greeks as small as possible. But when there is one-sided paper (i.e., all selling or all buying), position accumulation is unavoidable. When position greeks reach a certain point, traders will have to stop trading new opportunities that further increase their position—which is an unfortunate violation of the basic laws of economics. Generally, when buying, rational people want to buy more at lower prices (or sell more at higher prices) per a common supply-and-demand curve. But when traders keep buying (or selling) more and more, at some point they reach their limit of their risk thresholds and must stop accumulating.

Portfolio Risk Thresholds

Position risk thresholds are not additive. There must be some natural offsetting, or better yet, diversification for option portfolios. Just as investors attempt to diversify their investment portfolios, traders need to diversify their trading portfolios.

In the case of an investment portfolio, investors generally spread among sectors, such as technology, retail, foreign equities, and growth. But in the case of an options portfolio, traders must spread within and among the option-centric asset categories: direction, time, and volatility. In a roundabout sort of way, this is the same concept that applies to dispersion-model trading. Traders look at a portfolio as one big position, and they are always conscious of the master spread while making individual plays.

Traders must strive to take long deltas in assets on which they are bullish (expected market outperformers) and take short deltas on assets on which they are bearish (expected underperformers). Ideally, the trader will be directionally right on all trades. But it is not necessary for every trade to be a directional winner: it's a spread of sorts. If the broad market rises, expected outperformers ought to rise more than the market, and expected underperformers ought to rise less, making the spread profitable. Conversely, if the market falls, expected outperformers should fall less than the market would indicate; and expected underperformers should fall more—again making the spread a winner.

The same concept applies to volatility spreading. On individual positions, traders must take only long volatility plays when volatility is underpriced and short volatility plays when it is overpriced. Ideally, all volatilities revert to the mean, resulting in winners across the board. But, again, it's not necessary. If traders are making well-thought-out volatility plays, the spread as a whole should perform well with the goal that most will win while some will lose.

RISK-THRESHOLD BASELINES

How much risk is too much? That determination is somewhat subjective and contingent upon many factors, including the trader's capitalization, personal tolerance for risk, and style of trading. But there here are some baselines for position risk thresholds and portfolio risk thresholds from which to start.

Delta Risk Thresholds

There are two conventions for delta risk thresholds: normalized delta thresholds and beta-weighted delta thresholds.

Normalized Delta Thresholds

Being long 100 General Electric Company (GE) deltas is not the same as being long 100 Apple Inc. (AAPL) deltas. At the writing of this book, GE is an $18 dollar stock, whereas AAPL is a $330 stock. The nominal moves in AAPL stock are much more profound than they would be in GE—AAPL can move $18 in a week.

To normalize deltas, traders take the position delta and multiply it by the price of the stock. So, if a trader were long 100 deltas in both GE and AAPL, he'd have 1,800 normalized GE deltas (that's $18 share price times 100 deltas) and 33,000 normalized AAPL deltas ($330 times 100 deltas). *Clearly there's a big difference.*

In practical terms, traders must decide how many normalized deltas they are comfortable holding, given risk tolerance, capitalization, and other factors. For example, a trader may decide to set a threshold at 50,000 long or short normalized deltas. Thus, if the trader accumulates a position shorter or longer than 50,000 normalized deltas (from increasing options inventory or gaining deltas as a result of gamma), the position must be reduced in order to be brought back within compliance.

Beta-Weighted Delta Thresholds

Beta relates the correlation of a stock to the broad market, usually the S&P 500. A stock with a beta of 2 is expected to have a percentage move twice that of the S&P 500; a stock with a beta of 0.5 is expected to have a percentage move half that of the S&P 500; a stock with a beta of 1 should move in step with the S&P 500; and so on. Therefore, if deltas are beta weighted, traders can compare deltas on different stocks on an apples-to-apples basis, with the commonality being the relationship to the S&P 500.

Nowadays, many options platforms beta weight deltas for the trader. This makes position deltas very easy to relate to one another without traders having to import values into spreadsheets or calculate values by hand. Portfolio delta thresholds should always be considered in terms of beta-weighted deltas.

Theta Risk Thresholds

A trader can never have too much positive theta. It's the negative theta (i.e., losing money each day from time decay) that traders need to worry about. For both the portfolio as a whole and each individual position, traders must set a dollar-value limit for negative theta.

The risk threshold for portfolio theta is, once again, subjective and personal. But it should be observed as a percentage of the total portfolio value (including the value of all positions and cash). As a baseline, traders may set maximum negative theta thresholds between 1/2 percent to 1 percent of the total value of the portfolio— with 1/2 percent being more conservative and 1 percent being aggressive.

Each individual position must have a theta threshold set in dollar terms as well. This can be thought of in terms of a percentage of the entire portfolio or as a straight numerical (dollar) value arrived at through trial and error. Percentages for position thresholds should be significantly smaller than portfolio thresholds. Again, because traders should be diversified with some capital allocated to positive theta plays and some to negative theta plays, the value of each individual position is not necessarily additive to the portfolio threshold.

Vega Risk Thresholds

A similar philosophy can be stated about vega thresholds. But with vega there is no long or short bias; both positive and negative vega potentially represent risk of loss. Position and portfolio vega thresholds hold for positive or negative vega. Though subjective and personal, the following are some starting points for setting vega thresholds.

As with theta, vega thresholds for the portfolio should be set as a percentage of the total portfolio value. Though theta is biased, with only negative theta being unfavorable, vega is not. Positive or negative vega represents risk. Also, implied volatility may remain constant and is not a risk with the certainty of theta. Thus, the risk threshold for portfolio vega can be slightly more generous than the threshold for theta. A good baseline range is between 3/4 percent and 11/4 percent positive or negative vega—*with a caveat.*

Risk thresholds are maximum values. But each position should be contingent upon market conditions. For example, if the VIX (the benchmark index for market implied volatility) is uncommonly high, traders should not feel comfortable holding a position that approaches the maximum positive vega threshold for their portfolio. Risk thresholds are like speed limit signs; in addition to obeying the law, you'd better keep your eyes on the road. In other words, set limits for yourself, but let common sense and situational analysis allow for more stringent limits when a volatility position appears to have more risk than usual.

A healthy, volatility-diversified portfolio with accumulated volatility edge means that traders will hold positive vega positions in cheap volatility classes and negative vega positions in expensive volatility classes. So individual positions' absolute value of vegas may add up to more than the portfolio vega threshold. Still, they must be limited. Set vega risk thresholds for individual positions somewhat smaller than vega risk thresholds for the portfolio.

Gamma and Sliding Risk

The greek conspicuously not discussed, so far, is gamma. It is possible to set risk thresholds for gamma. However, there is a superior method for controlling gamma risk: traders should set limits for *sliding risk* (also called "up-and-down risk").

Positive gamma is always welcomed. But negative? Not so much. To be sure, small movements in the underlying asset are not a big deal. But negative gamma plus a big move in the underlying asset can mean trouble—*big trouble.* In fact, if traders aren't careful, it could be career-ending trouble.

With short option (short gamma) positions, traders can stand to lose much more than they stand to make. I've had students show me portfolios of income-trade positions that they thought were quite benign. But if the underlying asset moved 3 standard deviations, they'd have lost more than they had in their account. In trading-business lingo, that is called "blowing up."

Traders must look at their portfolio P&L given benchmark moves in the underlying asset, which is called "sliding-risk analysis." Some traders like to look at their P&L up and down one, two, and three standard deviations. Some, like me, prefer to consider the risk of big moves up or down in terms of percentage-move benchmarks. Conventional sliding-risk benchmarks are up and down 10 percent, 25 percent, and 50 percent.

Once a trader selects specific sliding-risk benchmarks, he or she must set a corresponding *pain threshold*, personalized to the trader. Pain thresholds determine the maximum acceptable loss to an entire portfolio given a benchmark move. For example, a trader may allow himself to lose 30 percent if the market moves (up or down) 10 percent, 35 percent if the market moves 25 percent, and still only 35 percent if the market moves 50 percent.

Because of the leverage of options, and the fact that this analysis is designed to help protect when only very large and statistically infrequent moves occur, the maximum allowable loss is presumed to be significant in a sliding-risk analysis. This technique is designed to specifically help guard against blowups. Complying with sliding-risk parameters ensures that negative gamma or biased deltas do not laden a trader with career-ending (i.e., irresponsible) risk.

The following baselines for pain thresholds corresponding to the benchmarks make realistic conservative starting points.

Benchmark	Pain Threshold
+/–10%	Loss of 20%
+/–25%	Loss of 25%
+/–50% (or more)	Loss of 30%

Thus, a trader adhering to this suggested sliding risk for his portfolio will not allow himself to create a portfolio that loses more than 20 percent if the market suddenly falls (or rises) 10 percent. If the market falls (or rises) 25 percent, the trader will have ensured that he doesn't lose more than 25 percent. The position will not be allowed to be big enough to lose 30 percent if the market suddenly falls (or rises) 50 percent or more.

Personalizing Thresholds

The baselines used in this chapter are mere ideas for starting points. Traders must find what works for them. Threshold values may be higher or lower than discussed here. Certainly these risks may be too great for some traders. Yet some may be not enough for highly speculative, experienced traders. And, again, they are limits. Traders normally ought to be significantly below set thresholds.

Note: Never change a threshold to accommodate a position(s) that has grown too big. Set thresholds based on sound logic *before* positions are established. Thresholds are law until the trader concludes that they don't offer enough potential to trade profitably, or that they are too lenient, which leads to the assumption of too much risk.

FIXING OUT-OF-COMPLIANCE PORTFOLIOS

When a portfolio violates risk parameters, it can be because of disproportionate risk resulting from a single option class, or systematic risk causing several classes to move toward violation. Traders should constantly monitor individual positions and their impact on the portfolio as a whole and address risk concerns when they arise. A single troubled position can be the bad apple that spoils the bunch. When one position can't take all the blame for putting a portfolio out of compliance, traders must decide between micro adjusting or macro adjusting.

Micro Adjusting Option Portfolio Risk

A trader's commitment to an individual trade is a result of edge, probability of success and risk/reward. But as time passes, or volatility changes, or the price of the underlying instrument changes; edge, probability and risk/reward change. A trade that was once a strong trade may not have the promise it once had. This type of trade should be weeded out, or at least reduced in size, to enable a trader to apply capital more competently on another trade.

When a portfolio is out of compliance with risk thresholds, traders should seek to eliminate the weak within the herd. It's like when corporations find themselves losing money: they must find the divisions that are not performing and make some cuts. With trading, when the whole account holds too much risk, eliminate the individual trades where risk is not being efficiently applied.

Macro Adjusting Option Portfolio Risk

Instead of changing the makeup of the components of a portfolio, traders may be able to adjust the risk of the portfolio as a whole. Traders can adjust the delta, gamma, theta, or vega of a portfolio by trading options on an index-based underlying instrument that are representative of a basket sharing similar risk to the portfolio. Or they can adjust just the delta with index-based options, futures, or ETFs.

For example, a trader with a large, diversified portfolio who has a long delta that violates his portfolio-delta-risk threshold may be able to hedge and come back into compliance by selling shares of SPY, selling E-mini S&P 500 futures, buying deep-in-the-money SPX puts, or many other ways. A trader who has portfolio vega that is out of compliance can buy or sell SPY or SPX options that have relevant extrinsic value, VIX futures or options, and more.

To effectively hedge portfolio risk, traders must ensure that they offset risks that are out of compliance while not violating other risk parameters. For example, imagine a trader's sliding risk at up 10 percent is too great for the set pain threshold and the trade is close to being out of compliance on positive vega. To hedge the upside sliding risk, the trader can buy an SPX call. But a long call might contribute to the trader violating his positive-vega threshold. The trader might, instead consider selling an SPX put.

The Perfect Hedge

Effective portfolio hedging requires creativity. Because most option trades have multiple risk attributes (of delta, gamma, theta, and vega), traders should plan hedges that address multiple risk attributes, always seeking to eliminate unintended risks. Traders must fit individual option trades into their portfolios like puzzle makers need to fit pieces into the puzzles just right. Further, they should strive to always gain volatility edge on individual trades. This is the ideal combination for optimal portfolio hedging.

For example, imagine a trader is long delta and vega approaching portfolio-risk thresholds in both. Ideally, before considering a macro portfolio-risk adjustment, the trader should seek to initiate a credit call spread on a stock on which he is bearish that has overpriced implied volatility. Thus, the trader reduces portfolio delta, reduces portfolio vega, and makes a smart trade with edge. Secondly, the trader could look to eliminate a debit call spread in inventory that no longer has a volatility advantage to the same effect.

17

THE SYMBIOTIC RELATIONSHIP BETWEEN THE MAKERS AND THE TAKERS

I often hear people in the media (specifically, people without real trading experience) say that the average trader simply cannot compete with the technology-laden, well-capitalized masters of the universe we know as market makers. On some occasions, I even get an earful of this from actual traders—usually novice ones. Market makers are often seen as the enemy. Is it because market makers are perceived to be the haves in a *haves-vs.-have-nots* relationship? Or is it simply the fear of what people don't understand? Maybe it's just a little displaced aggression. Whatever the reason, this unfounded demonization exists. But, guess what? Market makers often look at market takers the same way.

THE OMINOUS MARKET TAKER

"How did he *know*?" is a phrase I'd hear someone yell sometimes on the trading floor. (This phrase was often preceded or followed by creative expletives.) Admittedly, every once in a while it was I who was doing the yelling. We market makers would be standing around, minding our own business, when we'd make a trade and watch the trade instantly go against us for a big loss. It was like magic—*black magic*. How could the person on the other side of the trade have known that right then, at that very moment in time, the stock was going to take off?

The fact is, the trader probably did not know anything we didn't know. He or she just happened to be the beneficiary of some good, old-fashioned luck. But at the time, these sorts of coincidences surely seemed ominous. But luck is bound to happen from time to time. I've had it (good and bad) many times over in my career. Trades sometimes, by chance, went immediately and horribly against me; sometimes, by chance, they went immediately in my favor. And, surely when trades just happened to go my way and I was the beneficiary of luck, the retail trader on the other side of the trade cursed my kind with great fervor.

THE ZERO-SUM GAME

Option trading is not a zero-sum game. Neither side (market makers or market takers) cares much about whether the other side makes money or not. That matter is irrelevant. The only part of the trade that is actually a genuine zero-sum game is the chunk of change between the bid and the ask. That is, generally speaking, what the market makers would like to gain as profit. The market takers hope to give up as little as necessary. That's really all that market makers and market takers fight over.

Though the makers and the takers are on opposite sides of the trade, they have a common goal: to make money. In fact, I would argue that they—often unbeknownst to themselves—help each other. That's because the similarity between the two ends with their pursuit of the almighty dollar. Though they may be on opposite sides of the same contract, they are in fact trading two very different, and not necessarily directly opposite, things.

VOLATILITY TRADING VERSUS CONVENTIONAL POSITION TRADING

Market takers typically make their money as position traders. The bid-ask spread is just one of those costs of doing business that must be overcome. Market takers trade by taking either long or short positions directionally, or long or short positions on quasi-volatility trades that are generally traded as breakeven-analysis trades (in that case, the underlying instrument must remain within the breakevens on a P&L diagram or move outside them—in order to profit).

Option strategies traded by retail traders are necessarily intended to be high-profit trades. Even on somewhat conservative directional plays, retail traders hope to—and need to—make returns well into the double digits in just a short period of time. The percentage given up to the bid-ask and the possibility of leveraged losses demands that the winners have high percentage returns—and they can, because of their leverage. And on income trades, market takers hope to make much, if not all, of the maximum potential profit on trades. That also usually ends up to be a double-digit return on risk in a short period of time. *Market takers seek to exploit the leverage that options provide.*

Market makers construct positions out of the same options traded by their market-taking counterparts, but the positions traded by the market makers function entirely differently. The market makers' view of trading, even their nomenclature, is very different from that of the retail traders. Case in point: say the phrase "iron condor" to a market maker, and you're likely to get a blank stare.

In a perfect world, market makers ideally only want to trade the bid-ask spread (i.e., buy the bid, sell the offer, and go home flat). They want activity; they want liquidity; they want to trade in and out of trades all day long. The problem is, they can't. They can't go home flat every strike every day. There's not enough two-way paper. They end up acquiring positions. Market makers end up getting very good at managing positions because they are always taking the positions that the rest of the world lays off on them.

Market makers accumulate risk and reduce risk. That is their natural ebb and flow. They trade positions delta neutral; hence, they become volatility traders by necessity, as volatility trading generally has less risk than directional trading. Contrary to the philosophy of market takers, market makers hedge off leverage.

The philosophy of each party needs to be stated very clearly, and from each party's own unique perspective: Market *takers* make a living selling options (or option positions) at a higher option premium than that at which they buy. Market *makers* make a living by selling at a higher volatility than that at which they buy. Though, again, they may be trading the opposite sides of the exact same options, their differing trading perspective makes for a symbiotic relationship.

THE SYMBIOTIC RELATIONSHIP BETWEEN THE MARKET MAKERS AND THE MARKET TAKERS

The market makers' yin needs the market takers' yang: market makers provide the liquidity market takers need, and market takers provide the order flow market makers need. But the real symbiosis between the two is in the natural inefficiency of the volatility market that arises from these two parties trading with each other.

The Natural Inefficiency of Volatility Pricing

As mentioned, the market makers' goal is to sell a higher volatility than what they buy, and they would prefer to do so by buying the bid, selling the offer, and avoiding carrying a position for an extended period of time. They necessarily work on small margins; they are penny conscious.

For example, a market maker might take a long volatility position that has a 0.03 vega at a 32 volatility level and then sell it at a 34 volatility level, thereby locking in a 6-cent profit (0.03 vega times 2 volatility points). Market makers don't care if the underlying instrument rises or falls. It doesn't matter. That's not what they're trading. They're trading the derivative, not the actual security. They're trading for volatility points that are turned into pennies via vega.

Most market takers, however, don't care if they bought a 32 volatility level or a 34 volatility level. (Perhaps they should, but more often than not, they don't.) A few pennies usually don't even register on their radar. The way many retail traders think about it is that those pennies don't matter much to the results of each trade. *If I sell an iron condor and hope it expires worthless, does it really matter if I sold it for 2.90 or 2.92? If I buy a call at 2, does it matter if I sell it later for 5 or 5.05?* Many retail traders would say no.

Many retail traders completely disregard the volatility level. Surely, many retail traders don't know with any reasonable degree of certainty what volatility levels they are buying or selling. Even many of the best retail-based online options brokers list only one value for implied volatility in the option chain for each option. What is that number? The implied volatility of the bid? Of the offer? Somewhere in the middle? Is it representative of current market conditions? The implied volatility data available to retail traders are not nearly as precise as what professional traders use.

When retail traders trade with indifference to implied volatility, they create opportunities for volatility traders. All that indifference adds up. Market makers typically know down to a tenth of a volatility point exactly what the volatility of the bid and the offer are as well as their theoretical value. They must. That's what they're trading: volatility.

Supply and demand exist for each option that moves its market. But, mechanically, how that happens is through implied volatility. If the stock rises, a call price will rise not from demand pressure but because of the change in the relative moneyness of the option. If time passes, the call will get cheaper, not from supply pressure, but from time decay. Implied volatility is what truly measures the supply-and-demand influence on options.

Though implied volatility is often defined as *the market's expectations for future volatility of the underlying asset*, in actuality, implied volatility mechanically changes with buying and selling pressure. It is assumed (often wrongly so, in my opinion) that the buying and selling pressure is a result of the market's expectation for future volatility. But often the buying and selling pressure comes from retail traders trading and being indifferent to volatility levels.

For example, imagine that a popular options newsletter recommends that its subscribers buy unhedged, front-month, at-the-money calls in a particular series, say the Deere and Company (DE) May 90 calls, to speculate on the underlying stock rising. If the traders trading on the newsletter recommendation are interested only in call-premium-leveraged appreciation and not volatility, they will continue buying the offer, regardless of the volatility level. Implied volatility will then be bid up even though nothing has fundamentally changed about the market's expectations about future volatility of the underlying asset. The directional play will inadvertently affect, and cause an inefficiency in, implied volatility.

The volatility market is inefficient because of the number of market participants who are trading in the volatility market but are not trading volatility. This benefits volatility-trading market makers. It grows their business, and it grows their competition. They compete more fiercely for coveted mispriced volatility, thus ensuring tighter, deeper markets (i.e., more liquidity) for the market takers. It is a true symbiotic relationship. Therefore, it is my belief that options market should remain viable for a very long time.

18

PLAYING THE NUMBERS
Interpreting Options Data

You would never make a trade if you didn't disagree with the market. If an option is trading for $5, the only reason a trader would buy it is if he thinks it is worth *more* than $5. This is fundamental and should be common sense. Likewise, why would someone sell something at $5? Clearly, only because he or she thinks it is worth *less* than $5. Differing opinions create a market and propagate it with liquidity.

The reason different opinions exist in the market is because no one can see the future. No one knows for sure what is going to happen. So we all look for pieces of the proverbial puzzle to try and get a clearer picture of what is going on.

This is why analysis is so important to trading. We use technical, fundamental, and volatility analysis to get a clearer picture of each trading opportunity to understand what has been, and currently is, going on in order to position a trade to speculate on the future. One such bit of options data that helps traders understand what's going on is the study of *volume and open interest*.

VOLUME AND OPEN INTEREST

Volume and open interest are two kinds of options data that together, and in conjunction with still more information, help traders understand what is going on in an options class. Volume is the number of contracts that trade in a single trading day. Volume increases with each trade until the end of the trading day. At the start of each trading day, volume starts anew at zero for all options traded. Open interest is the number of contracts that exist, or are open. Open interest is a running total that continues on from day to day until the contract expires. Open interest increases and decreases as contracts are created (opened) and closed.

As one can imagine, volume and open interest can be useful information. Traders monitor volume and compare it to open interest to learn if contracts are being opened or closed. In fact, many traders use volume and open interest in just this manner. But to be sure, these two data on their own don't offer traders any useful information. To form a complete picture of what's happening in a particular option class, volume and open interest must be combined with more information—some of which can be known, and some of which, unfortunately, can't.

Comprehensive Volume and Open Interest Analysis

The first thing traders must work into a volume and open interest study is time and sales. Complete time and sales is a running time stamp of every bid, offer, and trade with its corresponding size.* With this information, one can get one stop closer to understanding what actually has occurred.

Imagine a trader, Bill, is monitoring options volume in Yahoo! Inc. (YHOO), which is trading at $15.90 in this example. Bill notices a single trade of 1,000 contracts trades in the March 16 calls one day.

---

*Many retail brokers don't offer complete time and sales. Streamlined versions usually consist of only trade price, trade size, and time.

Bill takes notice of this and consults open interest. He finds that open interest rose by 1,000 contracts that day. At this point, what does Bill know? He knows that someone initiated a trade to take a position in the YHOO March 16 calls. What can he do with this information? *Nothing*.

Did someone buy the calls? Did they sell the calls? Was it part of a spread? Covered call? Certainly no directional indication can be inferred from this limited information.

To get a better understanding of what has happened, Bill would want to know the price of the trade and whether the market taker initiating the trade was buying or selling. Why just the market taker? Because the market taker (e.g., a retail, institutional, or prop trader) is a position trader who is obviously making a big bet on these options. The market maker, who is presumed to be on the other side of the position trade, is simply absorbing liquidity and trading volatility.

Bill must consult time and sales. Upon looking up time and sales, he notices that at 12:02:41, a block of 1,000 contracts traded at 0.70 when the market was 0.65 bid, at 0.70 offer. Now Bill has more information with which to work. First, he confirms that it is indeed a single trade of 1,000 contracts. Second, he knows at what price it traded. But more importantly, he knows that it traded on the offer. Armed with this knowledge, Bill can infer that the market taker bought the calls to open a new 1,000-lot position.

The picture has become somewhat clearer. But can Bill trade off of this information now? He knows that there is someone, some-where in the world who bought these calls with great conviction; after all, a 1,000 lot is a pretty big trade. Does that mean that Bill should pile on and scoop some up to get long too? Not necessarily. What Bill doesn't know is the big trader's motivation.

Why is the big player buying these calls on an opening transaction? It's easy to jump to the conclusion that the trader is taking a bullish position on the underlying asset. But that may not be true.

Yes, the trade could be an outright long call purchase. But it could just as well be part of a spread—maybe a credit spread for which the trader has also sold the lower-strike March 15 calls. If that were so, that would indicate a moderately bearish expectation on the trader's behalf. Or it could be part of, say, a February–March calendar spread, indicating that the trader thinks the stock will be stuck in a range for the next few weeks. The trader could be a volatility trader who hedged delta neutral with stock. That would indicate the trader thinks either implied volatility is too cheap or that there exists a perceived gamma-scalping opportunity (i.e., the stock will be volatile). The long YHOO March 16 calls could even be part of a pairs trade in which the trader sold, maybe, Google Inc. (GOOG) calls or Baidu.com, Inc. (BIDU) calls against them. Without knowing the trader's motivation, Bill really doesn't know with certainty what to make out of the volume, open interest, and time and sales data.

The same could be said about a closing purchase transaction, an opening sale transaction, or a closing sale transaction. For example, if Bill observed that this call was an opening sale transaction, it could have been a naked call (bearish), part of a covered call (moderately bullish), part of a debit spread (bullish), or a credit spread (bearish). It is very easy for traders to trick themselves into thinking they are seeing something in the market when, in fact, much of it—often, too much of it—is veiled.

But there is an overriding superflaw to using volume and open interest data that is even more important than what has been discussed thus far. Even if Bill knew what the trader was thinking, *the trader could be wrong*. Many times retail traders perceive professional traders to be all-knowing oracles who know with certainty what the future holds. But they don't. Professional traders are generally fairly smart people. (Otherwise, they don't remain traders for very long!) But no one is perfect, and no one knows for sure what the future holds.

Analysis of volume and open interest is much like technical analysis using a stock chart and indicators. It doesn't predict the future. It takes available data and helps its analyzer better understand what has been going on, and what is currently going on, so he or she can make more informed decisions about the future. Analysis of volume and open interest provides important information, and I encourage traders to use it. But you'd better make sure you understand not just its strengths but also its limitations.

INTERPRETING IMPLIED VOLATILITY DATA

Much of this book has discussed implied volatility. It lies at the heart of option trading. To understand options, one *must* understand implied volatility. But here, again, is an analysis area where traders can ascertain important information but often trick themselves into thinking they are seeing something that, in fact, they are not.

The previous chapter discussed the inefficiencies of volatility pricing that results from the contrasting trading perspectives of the makers and the takers. Implied volatility is not *exactly* the market's estimation of future volatility, as it is often defined. It is unequivocally a measure of the supply and demand for options. Because implied volatility is high does not necessarily mean there will be a large, volatile move in the underlying asset. Low implied volatility does not mean the market will remain stable. For one, the volatility market is not efficient; secondly, even if it were, the market can be wrong.

Speculation and Protection

Market takers and market makers each have two different motivations for trading. They both trade for speculation or protection, but they do so in different ways.

Understanding the market takers' motivations is fairly straightforward. Generally speaking, they tend to buy options for speculation when they are looking for the underlying asset to move; they tend to sell options when they are looking for the underlying asset to remain in a range. This is generally true even with directional trades. Big moves profit more from outright trades than spreads. Thus traders will buy outright calls or puts when they expect a big move higher or lower, respectively; and they'll buy debit spreads—and, maybe even sell credit spreads—when they are looking for less volatile directional moves. Therefore, more demand pressure is injected into the volatility market when traders overall expect bigger moves.

The same scenario applies to selling pressure. Income traders play it tighter and use more protection (i.e., long options) when they have less conviction about selling volatility. The less they think the market will move, the bigger a negative gamma and negative vega position they are willing to accept, putting downward (supply) pressure on the market. Market takers hold in their power the control over the direction of implied volatility, though the precision to which they have an affect is inefficient and inexact.

But market makers provide liquidity by reacting to order flow. Understanding how they react based on speculative or protective intentions helps one understand liquidity and thus the potential magnitude of implied volatility changes.

Firstly, market makers mostly trade defensively, seldom seeking out a position in volatility or otherwise. When they accumulate a position, they itch to spread off the risk. Their position-protection worries can sometimes be seen in how volatility reacts. For example, sometimes implied volatility rises or falls faster than one would anticipate without any noticeable impetus (such as a rise in volatility preceding earnings). In these scenarios, the market doesn't absorb as many contracts on the bid or offer as usual. This development is evident in the smaller number of contracts on the bid or offer than usual; therefore, volatility must rise or fall faster.

For example, consider a certain, somewhat liquid option class that typically has 100 contracts both on the bid and the offer. Now imagine that the market becomes bid for 10 contracts and has 150 contracts at the offer and remains that way for a day or more. This scenario is telling. It candidly may be showing the market makers' hands. Market makers are obviously more anxious to sell volatility in this scenario. Why? Are they anxious to speculate on it falling? Not necessarily. More likely, they own a lot of options—too many—and are worried about their short theta and long vega. They need to protect themselves against the implications of carrying that risk. They are itching to get out.

Occasionally, market makers are a little more active in pressuring volatility, but their actions are usually preemptive rather than speculative. For instance, volatility traders need to be preemptive around observed holidays in which the exchange is closed leading to a three-day weekend. Market makers have an extra day of theta in which they cannot scalp gamma. Therefore, to protect themselves, they need to more aggressively lower their volatilities so as not to buy too many decaying options. They sometimes may be slightly more aggressive in these scenarios by trying to be among the first to lower their volatilities to sell options to get short vega before the expected decline in implied volatility.

Traders need to keep in mind what they can and can't decipher about high or low implied volatility. It does not predict future volatility—at least not very accurately. But, because volatility tends to revert to its mean, when volatility is above or below its mean—especially significantly—traders should try and figure out why. In doing so, they need to consider the psychology of both the makers and the takers. While doing a little digging for answers, traders just might uncover an opportunity to exploit mispriced volatility.

19

STORIES, SAYINGS, AND ADVENTURES FROM THE EPICENTER OF THE OPTIONS UNIVERSE

You can take the trader out of the pit, but you can't take the pit out of the trader. My experiences as a market maker on the floor of the CBOE have forever changed the way I think about things. I tend to assign odds to everything and view just about everything from a risk/reward standpoint.

I was out to dinner with some friends not too long ago. We were seated outside when the sky began to grow dark with rain clouds. The group of us began to discuss whether we should move inside. One of the people at the table suggested we stay outside because it wasn't supposed to rain until later. I couldn't believe it! We had nothing to gain by staying outside, only risk. *Perhaps, I go too far.*

Mostly, though, I already thought like a trader before stepping foot on the trading floor. Trading is very conducive to my personality and way of thinking. I've always only been certain about what I knew with certainty to be true: I've never been one to assume or take things for granted. I've always enjoyed solving puzzles. And I've always been fairly competitive.

ACTUALLY, IT IS WHETHER YOU WIN OR LOSE

That is one thing traders love to do: compete. In my career in the Chicago trading industry, I've seen, been a part of, or at least made some friendly wagers on just about every type of competition one could come up with. In the down time on the trading floor, there were feats of strength on a regular basis: push-up contests, running races, holding your breath—*anything you could think of.* There were food challenges to see how many eggs, White Castle hamburgers, or Big Macs someone could eat; how much milk or carbonated beverages someone could drink. And if that all got old, it was always great fun and an interesting psychological experiment to see how much money it took to get someone to shave his head. *That one ended up subsidizing many a clerk's salary.*

There seemed to always be a game. In the pit in which I traded, we would do brain teasers, ask each other what a certain number was in another base—for example, "What's 32 in base 7?" Game theory questions and obscure trivia always passed the time as well. For a while, we had a Scrabble board set up. *You really learn to play Scrabble strategically when you're playing against traders.* And, always, when the *Price Is Right* came on, we changed the channel to watch.

A prerequisite for anyone being a true competitor is being a good sport. *You can't learn to win if you don't learn to lose.* And, for the most part, our friendly competitions were just that: friendly. But every once in a while a dispute would break out (*note:* never with our Scrabble games; we kept an official Scrabble dictionary in the pit). When differing opinions escalated, every once in a while the conversation would end with someone proclaiming the colloquial challenge, "I'll meet you at the horse!"

Just outside the doors of the CBOE there is a large statue of a horse. That is where the fights were purported to happen. (I've never actually seen a real fight at the horse, however; *it seems the fun is in the challenge itself, not actually following through.*)

Traders need to blow off a little steam and keep themselves from getting too wrapped up in trading. This observation may come as a shock, but *trading can be a little stressful* from time to time. When I was full time on the trading floor, I didn't actually realize I was stressed at the time, though. *I loved it.* Only after leaving the floor did my wife inform me that I'm "so much more mellow now."

SLEEPING WITH THE TELEVISION ON

Market makers can't trade small. Expenses are too big, and besides, why waste the opportunity? *You're there for a reason.* Traders manage big positions that have big consequences. I can recall many sleepless nights thinking about a gargantuan short-gamma position that could surely be the catalyst to the end of my career if a surprise news story came out, causing the stock to gap. Often, I dreaded having to go to the floor the next morning; at the same time, I couldn't wait to get there.

HIGHER HIGHS AND LOWER LOWS

With trading, when you're up money, you're a genius. When you're down money, you're a fool. That's how others perceive you. And a lot of times, that's how you feel about yourself. It's a psychological roller coaster much more dynamic than what many other, nontrading people experience. Market makers get used to the action. They get used to making or losing tens of thousands of dollars in a day. *No biggie.* And so they get used to risk management.

Veteran market makers take no unnecessary risks; they always know their greeks and risk thresholds and always (try to) get flat before vacations, if not for the risk, then for the convenience.

I remember taking a trip to Arizona while I had several open positions, many of which were mostly long gamma positions on which I needed to enter hedges throughout the day. I was driving through the desert with my wife with a pen in one hand, a paper with all my orders written on it in the other, a phone on my shoulder, and my knee on the steering wheel. Wouldn't you know it, in the middle of giving the phone clerk an order, I lost cell-tower communication?—*being in the middle of the desert and all*. Note to self: trading is not a good way to spend your vacation away from trading.

But the life of a market maker is not always high stress. True, sometimes I'd come home, literally covered in sweat and spit, physically, mentally, and emotionally exhausted. But sometimes market making was just plain boring.

THE WAITING GAME: WHY (SOMETIMES) BEING A FLOOR TRADER CAN BE REALLY BORING

On TV, trading looks very exciting. But, that's because it's TV! Networks only show the busy days; *they only show the drama*. The fact is, when done right, trading *should* be boring. All market makers do is react. Ideally, they react logically, not emotionally, and they function very mechanically.

Sometimes, there wasn't anything going on in the stocks on which I made markets. Sometimes the whole market was slow. Because I had to wait for orders to come to me, there was literally nothing to do. I was like a store clerk sitting in a shop waiting for a customer. Except that there were a whole group of us in the pit all in the same predicament. How did we pass the time? See the previous section in this chapter titled "Actually, It *Is* Whether You Win or Lose."

When I started trading on the CBOE floor, about 90 percent of my trades were done in open outcry, with only about 10 percent done electronically. When I left the floor, it was just the inverse— about 90 percent electronic and 10 percent open outcry.

Back when the tide was starting to turn away from open outcry toward electronic trading, we used to muse about what would become of the trading floor. Among the top contenders that we kidded would make good use of the space were: museum, bowling alley, or paintball arena. Still, the trading floor does exist for trading.

But nowadays, the CBOE floor is even less active looking than it once was. The exchange is doing more volume than ever, but you can practically hear a proverbial pin drop on the floor. Almost all the trading is electronic now. Some traders still trade from the trading floor, but mostly it is done by sitting in front of a computer, quietly watching the screen. Probably, the exchange floor will remain home to traders for a long time, but just in a different way from days past.

Don't confuse a quiet trading floor with inactivity. The exchange is full of activity, with volume growing bigger and bigger all the time. But now it's cyberactivity. Traders trade from offices in the building and from offices far away. Traders dispersed geographically once electronic trading allowed for making markets remotely. I imagine many trade from places with a more favorable climate. Ever had to endure a Chicago winter?

GOODBYE AND WELCOME TO THE CLUB

When I first got started in this business, I got a *job* on the trading floor. As I grew in my career, I realized that it isn't just a job, it's a way of life. There's an options-industry culture that reaches far beyond the trading floor where I *grew up*. It's like a secret club that spans the globe. I've loved every minute of being part of the option-trading community. Through the good times and the hard times, it's been a great way of life.

I hope this book gave you a candid view of this industry, of which I am proud to be a part. I wish you, the reader, *the trader*, the best in your trading career. And . . . welcome to the club!

INDEX

ABOUT THE AUTHOR

Dan Passarelli is the author of the book *Trading Option Greeks* and founder of Market Taker Mentoring LLC™. Market Taker Mentoring provides options education, including personalized, one-on-one mentoring for option traders. The company website is http://www.markettaker.com.

Dan started his trading career on the floor of the Chicago Board Options Exchange (CBOE) as an equity options market maker. He also traded agricultural options and futures on the floor of the Chicago Board of Trade. In 2005, Dan joined CBOE's Options Institute and began teaching both basic and advanced trading concepts to retail traders, brokers, institutional traders, financial planners and advisors, money managers, and market makers. In addition to his work with the CBOE, he taught options strategies at the Options Industry Council.

Dan can be reached at dan@markettaker.com. He can be followed on Twitter at twitter.com/Dan_Passarelli.

AMITYVILLE PUBLIC LIBRARY

3 5922 00285 9050

332.63   Passarelli, Dan,
228   1971-
PAS
          The market taker's
          edge.

$35.00

DATE			

Amityville Public Library
Amityville, NY 11701

SEP 27 2011

BAKER & TAYLOR

AMITYVILLE PUBLIC LIBRARY